The *A*rt of Making & Marketing *A*rt Dolls

To Mary... Thank you for being such a good student and friend.

[signature] 10-7-95

Cover: Photo of "Norman Rockwell's Triple Self Portrait," 21" Cernit doll done by Jack for the 100 year birthday party. This doll is featured in the centerfold of the November 1994 issue of *Contemporary Doll Collector*. The doll is now owned by Franklin Mint. Jack considers this one of his best sculptures to date.

The Art of Making & Marketing Art Dolls

BY

Jack L. Johnston

WITH

Kathleen D. Ryan

ART DIRECTOR
Connie Carley

PHOTOGRAPHY
Jack Johnston

PUBLISHERS
Scott Publications

Special thanks to Russ Robison for the photography of "Norman Rockwell" and "The Fidler."

DEDICATION

"We only understand our full potential when our dreams turn to realities." This book is dedicated to Anne and Kim Mitrani, my loving mother Jane, and my sweet wife Vicky. Anne and Kim believed in my talent and encouraged me to become a professional artist, my mother believed in me, and my wife believed in my dreams.

My unfeigned hopes are that each person who reads and learns from my endeavor will see their dreams come to reality too.

Scott PUBLICATIONS

Copyright© 1994 by Scott Publications
30595 Eight Mile, Livonia, MI 48152-1798
ISBN # 0-916809-80-3
Library of Congress # 94-69313
No. 3852-11-94
PRINTED IN U.S.A.

A NOTE TO MY READERS

As an artist, I have illustrated characters and portraits for over 25 years. Only in the last few years have I added a new dimension to my craft—that of sculpting. With this third dimension a whole new world opened up to me, one that allowed me to truly create images locked and stored on paper or in my mind over the years. Sketches and drawings quickly took shape in clay. As my doodlings became sculptures, I knew that I had found the ultimate way to breathe life into those characters—I had discovered the art of dollmaking.

Starting as a beginning sculptor proved very difficult for me because no classes were offered in the area where I lived. Trial and error served as my only tutors. Though I progressed well, many questions plagued my mind. With great effort I resolved most problems on my own and eventually figured out the correct answers or procedures. Some questions, however, remained to haunt me in the quiet hours of early morning.

A pivotal point in my career occurred after contacting a professional artist I had met at a show, to ask her why little half-moon shapes kept appearing under the skin of my finished dolls. For months the answer to this perplexing problem alluded me. In desperation I finally posed the question to my fellow dollmaker, as one professional to another. Her reply was brief and curt. "Yes, I know what causes that, but it took me two years to figure it out, so it has become one of my trade secrets." Then, without another word she dismissed me, leaving me to struggle with the problem for several more months.

After that stinging conversation I vowed that I would never keep a trade secret from anyone who asked for my help, and I never have. Why should new dollmakers struggle for two years to know the answer to a problem if I can save them time and heartache by providing that answer today? Without cooperation between artists and prospective artists, the dollmaking industry would stagnate and eventually dry up, rather than flourish with the growth of fresh new artists.

If you attend my seminars, read my books, and view my videos, you will come to know as much about dollmaking as Jack Johnston. I hold nothing back. Sharing the joy and the knowledge of creating with others has become my lifetime passion.

Sincerely,

Jack L. Johnston

P.S. By the way, the solution to the little moon problem—never let the temperature of the oven go over 275°!

"The Left Handed
Fiddle Maker," 21"
Cernit doll by Jack
Johnston.

FOREWORD

In only three years, Jack Johnston, professional marketer turned dollmaker, rose from an unknown to one of the industries' brightest stars, astonishing doll artists and collectors around the world with his nearly instantaneous success. That his talent and artistic ability transcends every aspect of dollmaking is obvious. The excitement comes from knowing that Jack also possesses the ability to pass on to others, completely and successfully, that which he himself has mastered.

Just five months after sculpting his very first doll, Jack began sharing his techniques with others and began to successfully turn out a growing list of professional quality dollmakers. Averaging 42 seminars each year, Johnston travels all over the world conducting beginning, advanced and professional level classes in both Spanish and English, which cover everything from sculpting and costuming to marketing strategies. He also founded The Professional Doll Maker's Art Guild, an organization dedicated to perpetuating the art of dollmaking by assisting new artists in their quests to be professional dollmakers.

"I used to love to draw and doodle as a kid," says Jack, who graduated from Brigham Young University with a Bachelor of Fine Arts Degree in commercial art and marketing. After serving a tour of duty in Vietnam as a combat artist, he secured employment as a commercial artist. Jack loved his work, but it failed to provide enough income for his burgeoning family (eventually six children). Seeking a better means of support, he ventured into the resort marketing business where he applied both his commercial art talents and marketing skills. The combination worked and paid off handsomely. Jack rapidly became one of the industries leading marketing consultants, marketing resort projects throughout the northern and southern hemispheres.

In the twentieth year of his career, Jack was recruited as Vice President of Marketing for Dolphins Court at Sea World in Orlando, Florida. After spending only two years in this assignment, a slow down in the economy forced the lay off of 125 employees assigned to that project, including Jack. The timing proved catastrophic, as the family's savings had been depleted by the illness of Jack's youngest son who has leukemia. Because the economic slowdown was nationwide, Jack found it impossible to secure another executive level position in the resort industry. "There's no question that those were dark days for me. It was frightening. I knew that somehow I had to earn money to keep my family going," Jack said. Frustrated and desperate, Jack fell back on his art skill and began sculpting. In November of 1990 Jack attempted his first doll, a Father Christmas, which turned out so well he decided to display it at a local craft show. Not knowing anything about the one-of-a-kind doll market, Jack priced it at a mere $129. A fellow crafter snatched it up before the show even opened to the public.

Greatly encouraged by the tremendous response to his dolls, Jack sped up production while still maintaining his search for a "real job." But full-time dollmaking left little time to job hunt. It was not long before Jack made the monumental decision to become a professional dollmaker. By coupling his artistic ability with his marketing experience, Jack Johnston launched a dollmaking career which exploded at lightning speed.

Following leads and referrals into the electronic media, Jack landed numerous radio talk shows and a thirty minute special on PBS. The special is still being broadcast throughout the country. This coverage sparked enough interest to generate newspaper and magazine articles. From then on the telephone never stopped ringing with interest, orders, invitations for public appearances and other opportunities which most dollmakers only dream of.

Today, Jack teaches seminars internationally. He completed a book on dollmaking, produced a how-to series for TV, stars in a dollmaking video, signed a contract with Ashton-Drake Galleries of Chicago, Illinois, founded the Professional Doll Maker's Art Guild, and continues to make one-of-a-kind dolls selling for anywhere from $1,500 to $30,000 a piece. His works now stand as treasured art pieces in private collections and museums around the world.

TABLE OF CONTENTS

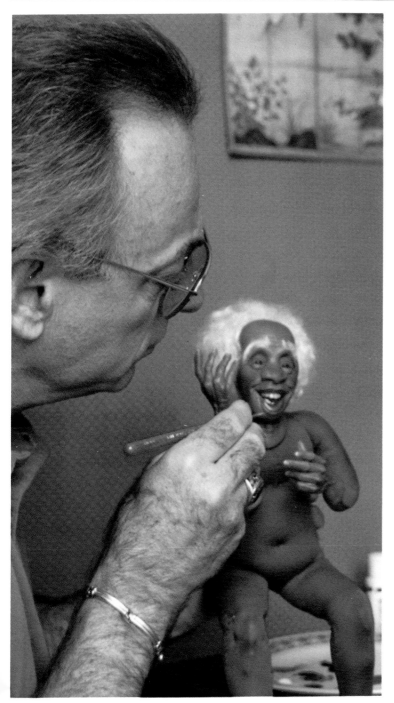

Jack Johnston painting the face of one of his sculptures.

My best work, "Mark Twain." This d
has been seen in all of the major d
magazines. It is in the Sedberry
Museum of Baton Rouge, Louisiana

CHAPTER 1

Introduction to Sculpting

You Can Do It!

No one can predict the heights to which you can soar, even you will never know until you spread your wings. You cannot discover new oceans unless you have the courage to lose sight of the shore.

When starting any new career, there are certain elements that must be considered. Dollmaking is no exception. In my travels I have met some very talented artists who, for one reason or another, fell short of making a living at their trade. I have also discovered many individuals with obvious talent who were completely unaware of their potentials as dollmakers. A detailed study of these various situations, coupled with my own personal experience, led me to develop what I feel are the five most important elements of successful dollmaking. Without any one of these elements, your chances of succeeding are dramatically reduced. With each of them in full force, success can be yours. You may be surprised at this list of elements and the order of importance assigned to them, but after reading this chapter you should be able to clearly determine for yourself whether or not you too can succeed at making and marketing your one-of-kind art dolls.

Desire

Many obstacles stand in the way of a person aspiring to become a professional dollmaker and everyone who tries may not make it. However, I sincerely believe that a strong desire is the first step to success. Desire fuels your efforts and keeps you going even when discouragement would drag you down. It clears away the obstacles and finds new pathways for you to explore. Desire grants you the will to continue until finally, in the end, you achieve. Anyone with a strong determination and desire to make dolls, who works at it single mindedly, can and will succeed.

Albert Einstein once said, "A lack of knowledge may be overcome by enthusiasm." I have amended that quote to read, "A lack of talent may be overcome by desire." Thus, I place desire as the number one key element in successful dollmaking, even before talent and ability.

While teaching a seminar near Philadelphia, I discovered that one of my students suffered a severe handicap which made it difficult for her to keep up with the other students. I suspected she might drop out of the class before too long, yet she persisted. Her desire to make dolls urged her on, forcing her to work even harder and more diligently than her classmates. When the other students complained about the difficulty of making ears, she asked for more explicit directions and pushed ahead. When I offered to help her sculpt she politely refused saying, "Just tell me what to do and I'll do it."

At the end of the first eight hour day when the others went home worn out, this determined student asked if she could borrow some tools so that she could work into the night. By the end of the three-day seminar, the undaunted artist not only completed her piece, but produced one of the best dolls in the class! Yes, she was handicapped, but not disabled. Why, because she had a burning desire to make dolls and to express and share her talent with others.

Oh! I forgot to mention the nature of her handicap. She sculpted with her elbows. Elisse Taddie has no hands or forearms.

If being successful at doll making is your burning desire, you too can do it! Never let doubt creep into your mind even if the process takes longer than you expected and proves harder than you anticipated. Often you may need to be inventive and stretch your creative abilities to their limits. You must also be willing to make sacrifices, for successful dollmaking does exact its pound of flesh. But if your desire outweighs the obstacles you encounter, a successful career as a professional dollmaker awaits you. Remember, with a strong desire, you will achieve and if your desire is strong enough, you will achieve greatly.

Time

Making a living as a professional dollmaker is more than a full-time sculpting job. Rather, it is a tremendously time consuming, labor-intensive effort, that demands total dedication and strict discipline. This fact struck home shortly after I made the conscious decision to become a full-time dollmaker. I recall mentioning to my family, "Now that I'm going to be self-employed I only have to work half a day and I even get to choose the half I want—the first twelve hours or the second twelve hours." They laughed because they thought I was exaggerating. I was not. If anything, it was an understatement.

Since there is no way to automate one-of-a-kind dolls, everything is done by hand. The process involves working with raw sculpting materials such as clay, tools, hair, eyes, fabric and wire, which must all be hand manipulated. I have shortened some of this time-consuming work by sending out my hand and body armature designs to be manufactured. The body stockings are also pre-made for me in four different sizes. Other than those specialized items, everything else on the dolls must be hand made, demanding huge amounts of time. Therefore, you must be prepared to rearrange your life to accommodate your doll-making efforts. You must also become inventive and learn to develop your own time-saving methods as I have.

The ability to multi-task, accomplish two or more things at the same time, speeds up your progress substantially. I will share some examples of how I multi-task to save time.

Warming polymer clay before kneading it makes sculpting easier and faster. I have found that sitting on the clay before I start to knead it brings the clay up to body temperature quite effectively. It may sound silly, but using this method to warm the clay frees my hands for other sit-down projects while the clay is softening. I use that time to shape the aluminum armature, thus accomplishing two tasks at once.

If you do not have the time to sit still, place the bar in a bag and put it in warm tap water (not to exceed 100 degrees or the clay will begin to cook) for five or ten minutes before you start to knead

Jack Johnston with a series of Santa Claus dolls.

the clay. Again, this offers you time to gather materials for the costuming, collect the necessary sculpting tools or even to load the dishwasher and make the beds.

In the evenings I find it very relaxing to sculpt while I sit and visit with family members or friends, catch the evening news, or watch a good movie on television. Again, this accomplishes several objectives simultaneously and makes each job even more pleasurable.

Sculpting while I am on the telephone serves as another time saver. So much of my day is spent on the phone conducting business, that I simply had to find a way to make better use of that time. Sculpting a head or hands is just like doodling to me, so when I am involved in a lengthy conversation,

I just grab some clay and doodle away. A humorous example of this occurred when I received a call from a seminar host to work out a schedule. We talked quite a while. By the time our conversation was over, I looked down to find a finished head in my hands. I had not even realized what I had done. It just evolved from my doodling.

I discovered another effective timesaver while making a line of Santa Claus dolls. Even though the dolls require different heads, hands, and clothing, making all the costumes up at the same time, assembly line style, really saves time. In one shot I design and cut out all the pattern. In another shot I sew them up. This saves money too because I can buy large amounts of material at one time.

5

There is no question that time can make or break the artist. Most artists are free-thinking spirits who move at their own pace, but as a professional dollmaker you must become more disciplined both in your business and personal life. I have pointed out the value of multi-tasking in the actual dollmaking process, but there are ways to squeeze out additional time in every aspect of your life by becoming more organized.

For over ten years I have successfully used the Franklin Quest day planner as my daily organizer but most any good planner will do. Here is how it works. At the beginning of each day I outline my daily tasks and prioritize each task to be performed. I assign a numeric sequence to each task, thus outlining the importance of completing each assignment before moving on to the next. As each task is completed, I write any special information to remember about that task in the diary, then put a check beside that task indicating its completion. If I have not completed a particular task by the end of the day, I move it to the next day and continue moving it from day to day until it is accomplished.

If a particular task has a low priority, it may be moved three or four times before being completed. If a task has a high priority, it must be completed before I finish the day. It is important to keep all tasks in your diary, not just your dollmaking business, but your personal schedule as well. This helps remind us of special assignments, appointments, etc., that our preoccupation with dollmaking would have us forget.

One of the best tricks to organization is knowing when you do your best. Are you a morning person or a night person? Do you function better under pressure or when you feel more relaxed? After this self-analysis, schedule and prioritize your work accordingly so that you are always at your best form while working each dollmaking task.

Remember, the element of time spent wisely makes the difference between success or failure. Sir Francis Bacon said, "Time is given in equal measures to us all. How we use that time determines the quality of our life."

Support

By a support system, I do not necessarily mean money behind you, although that certainly helps. The support system most imperative is the family and friends who understand what you are trying to accomplish and who will earnestly support you in the start up stages of the dollmaking business.

As outlined in the previous segment, it takes an inordinate amount of time to develop a line of dolls and get them in front of the public. You need people close to you who understand the kinds of sacrifices you must make in order to succeed—people who are willing and able to help support your efforts and even your absence.

For example, in preparing for a special show it is not uncommon to work in a flurry through the night, and then drive or fly off several hundred miles the next day, only to return just in time to change clothing and go out again.

During my third year as a professional dollmaker I logged over 180,000 air miles in 250 days. Your support system must see the vision of your work and your future just as clearly as you do. They must not only stand behind you, but allow you to lean on them when needed.

Trying to make dolls and run the new business alone is a monumental task. Yes, it can be done, but you will certainly be more effective and far less frustrated if you have physical assistance as well as emotional support. This aspect of support may come in the form of a spouse, an offspring, or a devoted friend.

Never hesitate to solicit the help of these people. In all likelihood they care about your success and are usually very willing to help in your dollmaking venture. In the early stages of starting your company, this type of help is imperative, economically as well as emotionally. Just knowing you have people there for you to help when and how you need it makes a huge difference. Put to good use all those who want to volunteer their services. Later when you start earning more money at your trade, you can hire outside help.

When I first started making dolls for a living, my entire family became involved and got me off to a running start. My wife made the costumes, one of my sons made hand armatures, another son kept track of my doll orders in the computer and another did the shipping and receiving for me. My parents helped by making the body stockings and armatures. They also took over the mail orders that came in for dolls and supplies. It took only a moment to ask for help and very little time to show them what I needed. The time they saved me freed me up to sculpt more dolls. As a professional doll maker it is imperative that you spend your time sculpting or selling. Some of the laborious tasks assistants can help with are: ordering supplies, shipping and receiving, correspondence, marketing, and public relations. As your assistants learn, they will also be able to prepare armatures and body stockings for your dolls, assist in soft sculpting the bodies, and help in costuming. The finished detailing, however, should always be completed by the primary artist.

In some cases, involving family and friends works out even better than you might expect. My parents, for example, became so excited about dollmaking and so involved in it that they eventually quit their regular jobs and started working full time with me in the dollmaking business.

Another good idea for support is to surround yourself with people who appreciate the magnitude of your undertaking and who love dolls as much as you do. Often these people are members of local doll clubs, organizations or shops. Not only can they provide emotional support, but also assist in your effort to seek out new ideas and find just the right materials or accessories.

In the beginning, much of your time as a dollmaker will be spent scouring the countryside looking for that "just right" accessory. I have learned that by involving my local doll club in the hunt, I save

time and often I obtain really unique accessories that I never would have found on my own. Most club members enjoy involvement in these little treasure hunts as it helps them feel a part of the finished doll, especially if they found the accessory for me. They can also help by offering additional input about what looks right and what does not. You will find most doll lovers quite eager to offer their opinions, listen and learn.

Soliciting the support of a doll club also affects your buying power as well, since ordering supplies together can greatly reduce your costs. Bulk rates generally run much lower than if you bought individually. For example, you can order 100 yards of mohair and pay only $2.25 per yard as opposed to the $8.50 you pay for each single yard. The same principle applies to eyes, clay, body stocking, armatures or anything else you might use in quantity.

Since doll club members are often artists and dollmakers themselves, they can provide valuable instruction to new sculptors. Make good use of this instruction. Everything I learned about dollmaking I learned the hard way— on my own. There were no classes available where I lived. Trial and error served as my tutors. For example, I must have made 35 pairs of hands before I realized that they needed armatures in them to give them form and shape and to keep the fingers from breaking off in shipment. Having a support system to fall back on like a club, a friend who sculpts, or even an instructor, is worth hours, days, or even years of the type of trial-and-error learning which I endured.

Knowing the difference a support team can make, you must now evaluate your own individual situation and investigate all resources available to you, to determine the best possible support system for the start-up stages of your dollmaking venture.

Talent

I am reminded of the tourist walking down the streets of Manhattan, pausing for a moment at the corner of Eighth Avenue and Broadway to ask a gentleman dressed in a tuxedo carrying a violin case, if he could tell him how to get to Carnegie Hall. The musician replied, "Yes, practice, practice, practice." The same principle applies to every form of art. To succeed, you must continually develop and build upon whatever natural talent you possess. Reaching your goal of professional dollmaking requires careful evaluation of your talent, a full understanding of what it takes to build upon that talent base, and practice, practice, practice.

It has been my experience that almost any persistent person can develop talent over a period of time. The problem is that most people are not willing to invest enough time in the learning process. As a result, many fall short of attaining a marketable talent.

For this reason talent lists fourth in importance on my list of elements, after a strong desire, support system and time management. I have found that anyone who wants to learn badly enough, who has the right support, enough time, and just a hint of talent, can and will learn the art of dollmaking

PHOTOGRAPHED BY: DIMENSIONS PHOTOGRAPHY

These are three of the first dolls made by Jack in 1990. These dolls are Cernit with soft sculpted bodies. They are in the permanent collection of Phil and Peggy Crosby of Winter Park, Florida.

So many students make one or two dolls and decide that they have no talent if the first two dolls do not sell. That is a serious mistake and an injustice to you as an artist. In the first place you should not even try to sell your first two dolls or even your first twenty. They are simply not good enough yet. To find out how to properly handle the clay, the tools and to perfect your skills, you should make hundreds of dolls. Obviously you have to start selling somewhere to provide the income to perpetuate your craft, but not until you have made at least ten to twenty heads. I have made over 2,000 heads and still learn something new almost every time. The most important thing to remember is that whether you are building upon a natural talent or developing a learned talent, practice and hard work will elevate that talent to a marketable level.

The next step is to objectively assess your talent as a professional dollmaker. If you find that difficult, ask others to do it for you. Consult your friends, family, members of a local doll club, doll shop owners, or other artists in your area. Try entering your dolls in small competitions. If you receive blue ribbons and lavish praise, then perhaps you are pretty good at dollmaking. But, are you good enough to earn a living from it? Remember the real test comes at the sales table.

After completing my first doll in November 1990, I felt confident enough to take it to a small craft show in Orlando, Florida. Knowing very little about one-of-a-kind dolls, I priced it at $129. It was such a steal that before the show

well enough to become professional. Two of my students from New Hampshire felt they wanted to make dolls professionally, but had convinced themselves that they lacked any real talent. They were afraid that their dolls would never sell—afraid of failure before they even began. Having already recognized a strong artistic talent in them early on, I considered it a personal challenge to convince them that they could and would achieve if they would just follow my directives and apply the five key elements of success.

I invited Kathy Wormhood and her sister Terry Eaton to take my advanced dollmaking class. After we concluded the advanced class, I challenged them to make four more dolls each. If those dolls

were good enough I would invite them to attend my professional dollmaking course. They worked long and hard. The beautiful dolls they produced easily qualified them for my professional class. Not surprising to me, both aspiring doll artists graduated in the top third of the professional class and exhibited their dolls to the world at The American International Toy Fair in New York, where they each received a nomination for the prestigious Doll of Excellence Award. Presently both artists enjoy the status of professional dollmakers, selling each of their dolls for $1,000 or more. Why? Because they worked diligently to build their confidence and develop their talents.

even opened to the public, one of
the other crafters bought the doll!
She agreed to let me keep it for the
rest of the show to take orders
from. In that first day I sold over
$1,200 worth of dolls and learned
two very important things: that I
possessed enough talent to sell as
many dolls as I could make and
that I was selling them too cheap-
ly. Both were pleasant realizations.

Assess the levels of your talent
and ability and use this book to
help build upon that base until you
too possess a marketable skill.

Marketing

Generally by the time we have discussed the four above elements in
my seminars, I have discouraged
90% of the would-be professional
artists. If you are still with me, and
feel you qualify in the first four
categories, you should know the
importance of effective marketing
in making or breaking your career.
It does not matter how good your
dolls are if you cannot sell them.
There is an old cliche in the advertising business that asks, "What
happens if you don't advertise?"
The answer, "Nothing happens!"

To help you better understand
the term marketing, let me define
it for you. According to the Ran-
dom House College Dictionary,
the term marketing means, "The
act of buying or selling, the total
of activities by which transfer of
title or possession of goods from
seller to buyer is effected, including advertising, shipping, storing
and selling." I wholeheartedly
concur with this definition, but
would add, "The ability to know
how and when to ask for the order,
coupled with the ability to know
when to speak and when to shut

Santa Claus entitled "Christmas Magic Worked Again." This doll is 24" tall and
made of Cernit with a soft sculpted body. It was nominated for the 1993 Dolls
Award of Excellence.

up." Many sales are lost by people
who undersell or oversell their
product. The fine art of marketing
and selling is a combination of just
the right exposure of your product
at the right time and in the right
place, followed by finesse in
securing the order.

After serving as a marketing
consultant for over 25 years, I feel
I have a fairly good handle on the
marketing of a product. If you too

have a talent for marketing, so
much the better. If not, do not despair. Marketing is not a science; it
is an art that may be learned. Just
as I believe anyone with a strong
enough desire can become a successful dollmaker, I believe that
anyone who desires to sell can
become a successful marketer.
Like making dolls, marketing also
takes a great deal of practice. You
must study your market and have

a working knowledge of what you can and cannot accomplish within that marketplace.

Do not be discouraged if you presently lack a working knowledge of how to sell. Being a natural born salesperson is just as unusual as being a natural born artist. To be born both is exceedingly rare. The ability to qualify your client, build value in your product, and secure the order takes some practice and a sound understanding of marketing techniques. You must understand that no matter how wonderful your product, marketing will make or break your company. Here are two sterling examples.

In my opinion, Xavier Roberts made one of the ugliest dolls I have ever seen and sold millions of them, known as the Cabbage Patch Doll. Mr. George Stuart, the finest Historical Figure® maker (a registered name he prefers over dolls) I have ever known, sold only a few of his figures to a museum. Robert's dolls are also in museums, as well as in nearly every household in America. Stuart's figures are relatively obscure, while the world renowned Cabbage Patch name made Roberts a multi-millionaire. The difference in these two situations lies in Roberts' ability to recognize the need for and to properly execute the marketing of his product. Mr. Stuart on the other hand has seen no reason to promote his work and is satisfied just seeing it in the museum.

I held this case up as an example, but time and time again I see cases of artists with equal talent, where one succeeds and the other fails or barely scrapes by as a direct result of marketing skills or lack of them. For this reason I devoted an entire chapter of this book to proper marketing strategies. When you are through studying it, you will not only have the ability to make beautiful art dolls professionally, you will also possess the necessary skills to properly market those dolls.

CHAPTER 2

Choosing Clay to Suit Your Needs

CHOOSING A CLAY
THAT SUITS YOUR NEEDS

Nearly everyone has at one time in their life sculpted something. Remember when as children we played with modeling clay and putty or made sand castles on the beach? We even sat in the bottom of shallow streams or puddles playing in the mud. Sculpting is just that simple and that much fun. Today's sculptors are no different than we were, playing in the river clay, just a bit more advanced using high-tech sophisticated clays. I am often asked what type of clay should be used in sculpting. There are several good answers to this question, depending on your purpose in sculpting and the effect you hope to create.

If you intend to make a reproduction mold of your sculpture, you may choose nearly any commercially available clay, be it natural or manmade. The favorite of most reproduction artists is plasticine. It holds its shape, has an extremely long shelf life if kept moist and cool, and can be added to or subtracted from. The drawbacks to plasticine lie in its color and finished appearance which are not conducive to beautiful stand-alone sculpture, but it was never meant for that. An artist using plasticine most often sculpts it into a finished piece, creates a mold from it, then destroys the original sculpture.

If you intend to make a mold of your finished piece, but would like to retain the original, you may choose a polymer clay such as Fimo, Promat, Sculpey or Cernit. These clays also boast a long shelf life if kept cool and away from direct light. From them one can sculpt a figure, make a mold, and complete the sculpture into a finished product that may be kept as an original prototype. Notice that I have not yet used the word doll when discussing sculpting with clay. That is because natural clays and polymer clays have been used for sculpting everything from human busts to models of cars for the automobile industry, even jewelry. As this book is written for the purpose of sculpting dolls, I shall now elaborate on clay for that specific use.

For many reasons, my personal choice of clay is polymer clay. In addition to its long shelf life, it is soft and may be added to or taken away from easily. Polymer clay may also be conveniently fired in a household oven. It absorbs paint and powdered color evenly, and is strong enough to be carved, sanded and smoothed after hardening. Most importantly, because of its wonderfully translucent quality, it naturally mimics the beautiful tones and textures of human skin.

Polymer clay, a manmade petroleum derivative called Poly Vinyl Chloride or more commonly known as PVC, is the same product that has been used for years to fashion plastic toys, jewelry, sprinkler pipes, patio furniture and even as parts for automobiles and airplanes. It can become an extremely hard substance or be very pliable, depending on the amount of plasticizer the manufacturer mixes into the formula. The polymer clay we use in sculpting begins as a soft clay, which when cured at the low oven temperature of 250°-275° degrees, hardens to a very strong, durable plastic.

Today's market hosts several good brands of polymer clay from Sculpey, one of the oldest, to Cernit one of the newer brands. Most polymer clay comes from Germany, with smaller amounts made in Britain, Asia, USA and Australia. Experimenting with each of them is the only way to know for sure which clay best suits your particular needs. They all work much the same in receiving color, curing, strength, price and finishing. The differences clearly lie in malleability and the finished look. Fimo offers the longest memory. By memory I mean that once sculpted into shape, Fimo tends to retain that shape. Inherently, because it is the hardest clay, it becomes the most difficult to knead. Cernit sits on the other end of the malleability scale.

While softest of the polymer clays and easiest to knead, it definitely displays the shortest memory. As a result, one part of the sculpture may shift while you are working on another part of the same sculpture. I overcome that by working with Cernit in stages. Sculpey's finished surface appears the dullest, while Cernit's displays the most lifelike and translucent qualities. Even though made by different companies, each polymer clay holds the same basic chemical makeup and therefore may be mixed together without any apparent side effects. As you become better acquainted with these clays, you may choose to mix them for different effects in either sculpting, coloring, or in the finished look. A combination of Sculpey and Cernit mixed together works best for me. The manufacturers of these two clays will not admit that the clays work well together, but

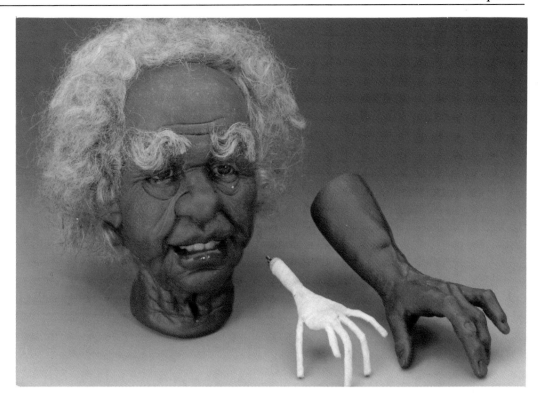

The world's first caramel colored doll made of Cernit. Jack was asked to design this color for the Cernit company. This "Black American Study" was sculpted by Jack for Handcraft Designs Inc. of Hatfield, Pennsylvania.

as they are both poly vinyl chlorides, they do. Their combination results in the easiest clay to use and a very fine looking finished product.

When I mix the two clays for malleability, it is usually 40% Sculpey with 60% Cernit. Fire the mix just as you would either of them separately. As both of the clays cure at different temperatures, I recommend using the highest temperature possible without scorching the clay. I use a temperature of 250° when I mix the two.

Mixing color in polymer clay is an acceptable practice. I have been mixing the three major brands of clay for years with very nice results. When mixing clays to produce a certain color, only you can adequately assess the percentages. First cut the blocks of clay into the proportions you desire. Then warm the clay by placing it in a plastic pouch in 95° water for a few minutes, or by sitting on the clay until your body temperature warms it to 98.6°. Monitor the temperature during the warming process care-

"Navajo Weaver" sculpted by Jack in 1993. The Cernit doll is 20" tall and wears a real turquoise and silver necklace. Her rug and weaving apparatus are authentic Navajo. She is filmed in the deserts of Utah, near her home.

fully, as clay will start to harden if the temperature reaches 120°. (For this reason also never leave raw clay in a trunk of a car.) Once the clay warms up sufficiently, knead it until the two colors blend together without a marble effect.

You may want to try this mixing process when working with flesh or bisque colored clay, as they are

"Pocohontas," this 30" Cernit doll is in the collection of Phil and Peggy Crosby of Winter Park, Florida. The basket in the hands of the doll is 150 years old. The beads are authentic to her Native American tribe.

generally too light in color for most dolls. The newest colors produced by Cernit are much richer and have very nice tones for the many hues of the world's population. I personally developed a new color for production by the Cernit company called Caramel. It is now available through most distributors of the clay. When using it to make a Black doll, you may use it full strength unless you desire a lighter color. In that case, mix flesh tone in until it becomes the color you like. Generally 50/50 to as light as 75/25 works for a lighter Black, Indian or Asian doll.

One drawback incurred when sculpting with polymer clay is the likelihood of air bubbles. It can generally be avoided by properly kneading the clay (a minimum of ten minutes) before applying it to the armature and then making sure to work out all of the air under the clay during the sculpting process. If you detect a soft spot under the clay, it may be eliminated by poking a hole in it, to let the air out. Then simply seal the hole shut. Of course, it is best to avoid this problem by thoroughly kneading your polymer clay before you begin to sculpt.

Since there are a variety of polymer clays on the market today, and you may choose to use any one or even a combination of these, *I will hereafter refer to any polymer clay simply as "clay."* Have fun experimenting with the polymers and choose the color and the clay that suits your needs.

CHAPTER 3

Equipment & Sculpting Tools

EQUIPMENT & SCULPTING TOOLS

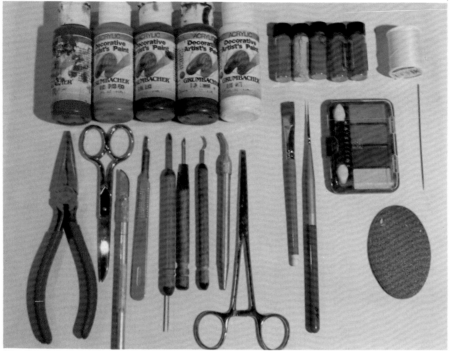

The tools used in Jack Johnston seminars.

My first one hundred dolls were crafted with an old crochet hook, a broken needle, and a very dull paring knife. As I progressed and gained a little sophistication, I added to my collection the smooth end of a fountain pen, a sanded Popsicle stick, and a set of used dental tools. Not until I began teaching, did I learn of sculpture tools commercially available at ceramic studios. These ceramic tools suit our dollmaking purposes quite well. However, some need to be smoothed and polished for maximum effectiveness in sculpting. In the above photo I have shown the basic tools which I recommend. Each tool should be sanded to eliminate any jagged sharp edges or burrs. Depending on your budget, you may purchase these tools all at once or improvise while you build your collection one piece at a time.

Primary Sculpting Tool

The first and primary tool you will need for sculpting dolls is the cleaning tool. All the major manufacturers of ceramic tools make this instrument with the same basic shape, therefore I have no preference to brand names. The modification to the cleaning tool is very simple. Grind down the end and edges of the tool to make it smooth and less likely to cut the clay, then highly polish the tool with jeweler's rouge and a soft buffing wheel.

The Lacing Tool

The second tool I suggest is the lacing tool or ear tool, primarily used for making ears. I also find it useful around the mouth, eyes and other tight spots. Again, the same design is used by all ceramic tool manufacturers. Grind the end of this tool to a smooth finish as

shown in the illustration. Then polish the surface.

The Fingernail Tool

Tool manufacturers refer to this instrument as the nail tool. Grind this in the same manner as the other tools to ensure the smoothest possible finish.

The Eye Shaper

This tool, used for shaping the eye sockets, is nothing more than a one-half inch or twelve millimeter dowel. Cut a one-half inch dowel five inches long and smooth the working end flat. The other end should be rounded to fit in the palm of your hand.

Two Knives

Your primary cutting and carving tool should be a one-half inch handled craft carving knife such as an X-Acto knife. Its blade must be convex (curved outward). A straight blade will not carve your clay effectively and might cause you to cut yourself when carving on cured clay. The carving knife is also used to cut away large amounts of raw and cured clay throughout the sculpting process.

The second knife you will need is a medical scalpel. For this I also prefer a convex blade. It works well to trim off pieces of clay from the sculpture during the rough finishing process, while the clay is still soft. Once the clay is cured, you only use the larger knife; the small one will break. Using either of these knives can be very dangerous. The medical scalpel is the sharpest knife available. It is sharper than a razor blade so please be very careful.

The Hemostat

This instrument may be purchased at medical supply stores. It is used by doctors to clamp off veins and arteries. In dollmaking we clamp them onto the wrists to hold the hands in an upright position while sculpting them. Because they are made of stainless steel, they may go right into the oven and continue to hold the hand during the curing process.

Glue Gun

This will serve as your main tool for costuming. Glue guns are quick and easy with many different models available. I strongly recommend one of the newer hot glue guns that heat at lower temperatures and thus avoid the potential of a serious burn.

Other Necessities

I incorporate so many household and workshop items into my doll-making, that it would be impossible to list them all. Whenever a special need arises, I poke around until I find a tool to do the job. Some of the more common items are sandpaper of varying grades, screwdrivers, regular pliers, needlenose pliers, scissors, awl, jeweler saw, jigsaw, hack saw, high speed electric drill, assortment of drill bits, a small table vice, lacquer thinner, cotton swabs, clean-up towels, clear fingernail polish, and spray fixative. I put all of these things and more to good use while dollmaking.

Paint Brushes

I use only acrylic brushes for those spots that require painting. When purchasing your paint brushes, buy only quality brushes. You may not recognize quality brushes when you see them, but will when you pay for them. A good brush costs about the same as a good meal. Remember, properly cleaning your brushes will ensure their life and effectiveness.

Aluminum Foil

Regular weight household aluminum foil works nicely for armature needs.

Paints and Colored Powders

Acrylic paints, china paints, and ladies' facial makeup are the colors most often used on my dolls. As with many great discoveries, I stumbled onto makeup quite by accident. During one of my early seminars a student discovered a strange color on her unfinished sculpture. Unable to determine its source, I noticed that it resembled the same lovely rose as her own face. As I watched her work, I observed her repeatedly reach up and touch her face. That solved the mystery. Clay picks up anything with color in it. Unaware of this, she transferred her own face makeup to the face of her doll through touch. Since her doll's face was already contaminated with the color, we decided to experiment with more of her makeup. I carefully brushed it on the cheeks and eyes of the doll just as a woman applies makeup to her face. It worked. In fact, it worked so well that we went straight out that very day and bought "Cover Girl" for the other students to apply. Impressed with the ease in which wet clay absorbed facial makeup, I adopted the use of it (despite funny looks from the cosmetic clerks) and have used it ever since with wonderful results.

Water based acrylic paint is essential for painting on polymer clay, remember PVC is plastic. As the clay is not porous, oil paints will not dry well. I use only water base paints for my dolls. The brands of paints and the colors vary so much that I do not want to try to list them all. I do recommend generic colors for you to choose from: White, black, crimson, yellow ocher, burnt umber, raw umber and royal blue. With these basic colors you can mix any color you like. If you do not feel comfortable with mixing, you may buy colors pre-mixed, such as flesh colors. One caution when buying your colors, always sample them on a piece of clay first. Some paints on the market will never dry on your doll. Make sure the ones you choose will.

The powder I use is nothing more than ladies' facial makeup, available at any drug store or super market. The only caution I offer is not to buy makeup with gloss in it. It must be matte. A simple method of checking this is to try some on the back of your hand. Most make-up has gloss in it so you may have to search through the display rack to find one without. Pastels work very well, but again a caution: Apply lightly to wet clay as they have a tendency to be too dark. Later in the painting section of this book, I advise on the best ways to apply makeup, paint and pastels.

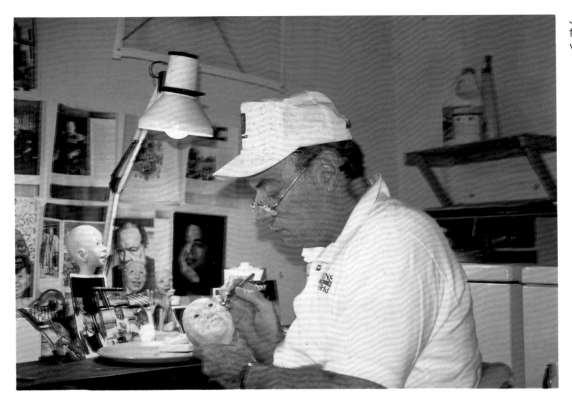

Jack working in his first studio, (a converted washroom).

The Studio

Studios can range in size from a converted closet to a purposely built studio. Since most of your time will be spent here, it should be spacious enough to suit your needs, but not waste space. When I started sculpting, I converted the washroom of our house into a studio with wall shelves to hold supplies, a built-in waist high table and a stool. My entire work space including storage totaled only about 30 square feet. Before long my dollmaking venture oozed into the dining room, eventually taking it over. This worked for about six months, until finally I expanded my business to a commercial building (actually, my family kicked me out).

I rented a 500 square foot office with a large table at one end and plenty of cabinets and drawers for

storage. I used two, three by ten foot worktables for sewing, assembling dolls and shipping. As my business grew, I took on another 400 square foot office and shared a shipping dock for receiving. Teaching classes was the next natural expansion to my business. That required another 700 square feet for classroom space.

If I were to design the perfect studio, it would be similar to that of Norman Rockwell's studio in Stockbridge, Massachusetts. I had the pleasure of visiting Mr. Rockwell's studio while sculpting my "Norman Rockwell Triple Self Portrait." This ideal studio housed in a two-story 1,250 square foot building is an artist's dream. Glass windows shoot up two stories to an open beamed ceiling. A cozy loft looks over the studio offering space for research books and stor-

age. The studio bathroom stands in the center of the building surrounded by several large rooms where Mr. Rockwell kept props and other storage items. I would make the largest room a classroom for teaching and the loft a computer and communications center.

Because I handle all of my own correspondence and advertising, I spend as much time on my computer as I do sculpting. Therefore, I believe the ideal studio should consist of a sculpting room, a computer room, a spacious sewing area, a shipping and receiving facility, a library for resource materials, storage shelves and cabinets for cloth and doll supplies, a restroom with separate hand washing facilities, and a classroom for teaching. This classroom should contain a table large enough for

Jack's purpose built studio.

fifteen students (the maximum size for effective teaching) and each workstation on the table should be set up like a mini studio. The ideal studio should include many electrical outlets, good ventilation, direct overhead lighting, a stand to hold sculpting tools, and a place for paints, brushes and a palette.

No matter what size sculpting studio you choose, remember that the main objective is to have everything you need at your fingertips. Hunting for supplies or that special tool takes up too much

of your time and when you are making dolls for a profession, time is money. Do not imagine that to successfully make dolls you can only function in the ideal studio described above. That studio can come along later or not at all.

Some of the best dolls I have ever made were sculpted in front of the TV set while sitting in a soft

chair. But, if you have a choice, make your studio as nice as you can afford. After all, you will work and think better in a comfortable efficient environment.

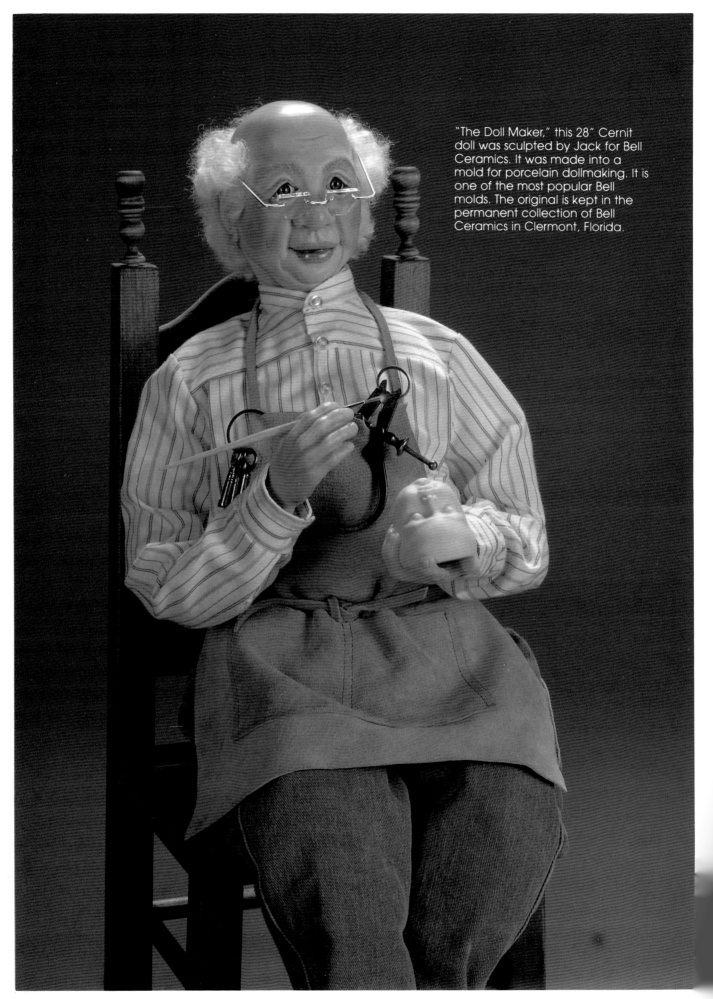

"The Doll Maker," this 28" Cernit doll was sculpted by Jack for Bell Ceramics. It was made into a mold for porcelain dollmaking. It is one of the most popular Bell molds. The original is kept in the permanent collection of Bell Ceramics in Clermont, Florida.

CHAPTER 4

Special Effects

Photo of the "Vision Quest." These two Indians are 20" tall, made of Cernit, and costumed in real leather, furs, and authentic jewelry.

35mm Camera

It may appear odd to list a camera as part of the necessary equipment for a dollmaker, but in reality it will become one of your most important tools. I have photographed each of my dolls, since doll number one, for several reasons. Keeping an accurate photographic chronicle of your work helps you to evaluate your progress and spot weak areas. Sometimes the camera picks up what escapes the naked eye. We may squirm at the sight of our mistakes, but these photos teach us and mark our progression.

Quality photographs are absolutely imperative for featuring your work in ads or magazine articles. When editors consider doing a story on a particular artist, professional quality photos are the first thing they ask for. More often than not, their decisions to go with one artist or another rests solely on who supplies the best photographic artwork. It makes all the difference. Most of us have seen a photo of a doll, compared it to the actual doll, then realized that the photo either made the doll look much better or much worse. Good photography increases sales. Many dolls net top prices from a photo alone. This is especially true for one-of-a-kind art dolls, where the doll may be thousands of miles from the prospective buyer. Likewise, a bad photo could cost you that sale. In this highly aesthetic business, a picture truly is worth a thousand words. I cannot stress enough its value.

Photography is an art form just like dollmaking. In fact, learning to properly photograph your dolls

Photo of "Winston Churchill." This is the first commissioned doll made by Jack. It is in the permanent collection of Phil and Peggy Crosby of Winter Park, Florida. The hat and the doll are made of Cernit. The costume was hand-made by a Chinese tailor. It has pockets, buttons, lining, fly, and a working gold watch.

may demand as much talent as making them. But I assure you that in the long run it pays off handsomely and is well worth the time it takes to learn. Remember, many gifted artist's careers have sky-rocketed or toppled based on the quality of their photographic representation.

Ideally, I would recommend a large format camera (120mm) such as a Hasselblaud. All of the magazines prefer large format transparencies for their color work. For those beginning artists who cannot afford a large format, a good 35mm will work too, as long as it is a quality camera and lens.

Your camera should be equipped with a 35mm to 70mm lens, tripod and lights. The 35mm wide angle lens works great for closeups, while the 70mm telephoto shoots best outdoors. The telephoto lens draws the background into the picture and makes everything appear in scale. You will also need a seamless backdrop for inside shots and at least two photo flood lamps. Strobe lights work best but are not imperative. For a limited budget use photo floods. One tip when photographing your doll, always get down to eye level with the doll, making certain that everything in the photograph appears in scale.

Notice in the photograph of 'The Vision Quest" how realistic the photograph makes the dolls look. To get this shot, I traveled to the top of the mountains, waded in snow up to my waist and waited a half a day for the sun to hit just right. I often spend an entire day preparing for a shot or go through two or three rolls of film just to get one perfect picture. This may

sound like a lot of work and money, but I learned to spare no expense when it comes to great photography. I spent $500 creating a set to film "Mark Twain." It included special effects lighting, designed to imitate the sun. Rays of this light burst through the windowpane, shot-crossed the floor and splashed on the doll's trousers. It took two days to get this perfect shot. Was it worth it? Well, the finished product landed "Mark Twain" in *Doll Crafter* magazine and netted me one full year of seminar bookings. Any more questions?

Costumes and Accessories

Nothing polishes off a good doll like a great costume and stunning accessories. The right touches can make a poorly sculpted doll look wonderful, while a great sculpture might be ruined with bad costuming and accessories that are out of scale. As appropriate costumes and accessories are a fetish of mine, I will explain the fine nuances that go into finishing off the doll properly. Many times these details are so important that I work on them first, before I begin to sculpt the actual doll, as in the case of "Sir Winston Churchill."

When I received the order for my very first portrait doll, "Sir Winston Churchill," I immediately set out to search for just the right pocketwatch, even before sculpting the doll. Authenticity demanded a real gold watch, perfectly in scale, that kept accurate time. It seemed an impossible venture. Eventually, I did find the perfect watch but it was too large. How to solve the problem?

I work in a scale of two-and-one-half inches to three inches equals one foot. This scale is much larger than "standard miniature" (one inch equals one foot) but it fits comfortably for my dolls. However, finding scale accessories and costumes becomes more difficult. Often I spend as much time looking for these items as I do making the doll. This particular watch I found was even larger than my large scale. The problem resolved itself when I decided to make "Winnie" fit the watch by sculpting a bigger doll than normal. Finding the watch first allowed me that flexibility. As a result "Winnie" stands about six inches taller than my other dolls, but the watch remains in perfect scale, making a good case for finding the right accessories before sculpting the doll. You never know what adjustments you might need to make.

"Winnie" required a special bowler-style felt hat in perfect scale. As I suspected, such a hat was not commercially available so I designed and made one myself. The same situation arose with the essential wing-tipped shoes. I solved that problem by sculpting the shoes out of clay, cutting real leather soles and dressing them up

The "Mountain Man," stands 21" tall and his costume is leather with real furs. The snowshoes are authentic antique salesman samples.

with string laces. The result proved so realistic that you actually had to touch the shoes to determine that they were not fine quality leather shoes. His three-piece suit presented another challenge. After an exhaustive search, I finally found a willing tailor with the right color material, in a small pinstripe. Using the doll as the mannequin, he designed a miniature suit delicately detailed with pocket lining, buttons sized to scale, and a fly just like a real suit. It cost about the same as a real suit too, though I never regretted paying the $250, as the doll sold for $1,000. Three years later, "Winnie's" value sprang to $8,000 and continues to climb each year.

Once, while walking through an antique store, I happened upon a pair of antique snowshoes in scale. Made as salesman samples, they

were a rare find indeed. I bought them not even knowing what I would do with them. Some three years later I made my "Mountain Man" as pictured above. Nothing could have set him apart better than those snowshoes. I paid over $100 for the shoes, but as you can see, they absolutely made the finished doll. His accessories also include a scale rifle and Bowie knife crafted especially for him. I cut the costume from deer hide and rabbit pelt as fitting for a man in that era. I believe this doll to be one of my best pieces, primarily because of the wonderfully authentic accessories and costume.

The following photo of "Mark Twain" displays my most elaborately accessorized doll. I spent one year creating this piece and collecting just the right accessory items. My good friend and master

...hoto of "Mark Twain." The doll is 20" tall, Cernit with a soft sculpted body and surrounded by authentic working acces-...ories. All accessories were hand-made by Dennis Dugan of Alton, Illinois. Jack considers this doll to be one of his finest.

...raftsman, Dennis Dugan, built the ...rniture for this doll. Notice the ...esk, cabinet, and chair are all in ...erfect scale. The drawers in the ...rniture all work, the doors open ...nd close, and the chair actually ...wivels and rolls. The books all ...ave type in them, the lamp on the ...esk features an adjustable wick ...nd burns coal oil. The authentic ...ewspaper was printed as a sales-...an sample near the turn of the ...entury. The main drawer of the ...esk holds all the junk one would

expect Mr. Clemens might have tossed in there, such as extra pens, paper, a pocketwatch, a pocket-knife, several coins, cigars and other very special items. The clock, a beautiful replica of that era, keeps accurate time. I spared no expense accessorizing this doll. Judge the results for yourself. You may visit "Mark Twain" on perma-nent display at the Sedberry Doll Museum in Baton Rouge, Louisiana.

Learning to make costumes pre-sented the biggest challenge of all to me. When I first started sculpt-ing dolls, I had absolutely no knowledge of how to sew and con-sequently relied on my support team to construct the costumes. Later when volume increased, I hired out the work to costume makers from around the country, but ended up paying as much for the outfits as for the actual doll. Even at those high prices problems remained. Many times the costumes came back out of scale, the wrong style, or just not to my specifications. By the time we finished shipping the garments back and forth, the doll cost more in terms of time and money than I ever anticipated. This forced me to attempt my own costuming, even though a sewing machine and I were perfect strangers. After a brief introduction and a rocky courtship, we settled down to a comfortable working relationship. Design and pattern making followed naturally. Unfortunately, even though the machine stitched as small as 24 stitches to the inch, it was noticeably too large for scale. Hand sewing was too difficult for me and way too time consuming, so I ruled it out. Driven by desperation, I experimented with glue and quite surprisingly discovered glue to be a dollmaker's best friend.

The "National Institute of American Doll Artists, NIADA" offers its definition of an acceptable doll as; human like, wearing clothing that appears to be undressable. The key word here is "appears." My dolls from 1990 until 1993 were undressable, but someone else made most of the costumes and they often cost more than the doll. Today, thanks to glue, the costumes look much better, are designed and made entirely by me, and cost a fraction of what I was paying. But they cannot be removed without totally destroying the doll. Now I sew only areas that need stitching for effect or to finish off large areas faster. Everything else, I glue. It's a bit sticky, but with practice you can become so refined in your gluing technique as to make perfect collars, lapels, and even French cuffs.

There are several good glues on the market. Any fabric glue from your local fabric store or white glue will work. I prefer electric glue guns. They are easy, fast, and the new cooler temperatures reduce the threat of burns. However, you must work very quickly because this glue sets almost immediately. One of the tricks when applying any glue, is to use it sparingly. Try not to get the glue too thick or let it show at the edges of the seams.

Of course, the most important factor in costuming is the fabric you choose. I select nearly all of my well-worn fabrics from used clothing stores, antique shops, and my own closet. In fact, when I purchase a new shirt I think how it will look on a doll later when I am through wearing it. The fabric must be thin and very tightly woven to properly drape on your dolls, with prints and designs in scale. If using leather, it must be extremely pliable and thin too. The very best leather is "kid leather." The best source of kid leather is ladies' hand gloves. They are readily available at garage sales and second-hand outlets. Do not overlook your grandmother's attic. Look for treasures such as old laces, handkerchiefs and napkins. You may even get lucky and find an old fur coat or a kid leather vest. Kid leather coats or fine furs from young animals are rarely made anymore because of the animal activists, but I think it best to use these old pelts when needed for effect in dressing a period doll rather than letting them just lay in a chest somewhere.

For costuming authenticity I recommend you research period clothing to identify appropriate dress. Libraries offer mountains of information as do museums and videos. Watch old movies or thumb through period picture books for more realistic design and accessory ideas. Libraries also offer volumes of books on design and pattern making. Or you may purchase these guides in craft or bookstores. Doll shops or clubs can provide valuable information along these lines as well. Accuracy and detailing in period clothing and accessories increases the value of your doll. The more realistic your workmanship, the greater the value of your doll.

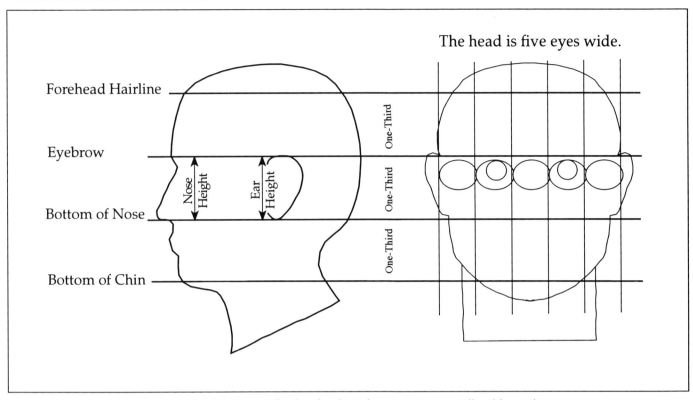

The head is five eyes wide.

Forehead Hairline

Eyebrow

Nose Height

Ear Height

Bottom of Nose

Bottom of Chin

One-Third

One-Third

One-Third

Comparative head sizing chart. Used in proportioning forehead, eyes, nose, mouth, chin and ears.

thumb to apply to proper proportions, beginning with height. The masters of sculptured and drawn figures seem to have a difference of opinion concerning the size of the human figure. Michelangelo sculpted his figures nine to ten heads tall. Many of Raphael's sculptures are as small as six heads high, while Auguste Rodin's figure stands a perfect seven-and-one-half heads. I have found the most realistic dolls to be at seven heads. Any less, gives the doll a caricature or cartoonish look.

Actual proportions may also vary with the age of the subject. For example, a four-year-old is only five heads high. By the time a child reaches the age of sixteen, he or she will likely be seven heads high. The head will only increase in size from a child to an adult by about thirty percent, whereas the body will increase by over two hundred percent. This phenomenon creates so many variables in size relationships that it would be very confusing to attempt rules of

thumb for every age. Therefore, I will only cover the rules for an adult. Since the average human adult stands seven-and-one-half to eight heads high, I will use these figures as our measurements for realism.

An adult body can be evenly divided in half at the crotch. It measures three and three quarters heads high from the top of the head to the bottom of the crotch and the same from the crotch to the bottom of the feet. The upper torso, including the head, measures the same height as the legs including the feet.

We generally divide a person's head into three equal parts.
1) the hairline down to the forehead
2) the eyebrow to the bottom of the nose
3) the bottom of the nose to the bottom of the chin

The ears are the same height as the dimension between the eyebrow and the bottom of the nose. The mouth in its relaxed form is

the same width as the distance between the inside color of the eyes. Extended into a full smile the mouth measures the same width as the outside color of the eye. The ear holes are situated in the center of the head from front to back and from top to bottom, with the flower of the ear in the rear one-half of the head.

Imagine a skeleton under the skin of each head you study. This will help you understand why facial structures appear as they do. Notice how a person's weight affects facial features. The eyes, chin, cheeks, and even the mouth can be completely altered with the loss or gaining of fatty tissue. A fat person has the same muscles in his face as a skinny person, yet the very weight of the fat tissues will show age faster as gravity pulls on the skin. Age will elongate the ears and nose, and at the same time shrink the chin as the teeth wear short. A youthful face will appear more like a round ball due to the fatty tissue and the fact that gravity

29

has not taken its toll.

Observe that a person with a small nose has small ears as well and a person with wide set eyes, features a wide mouth. Be aware of how the eye fits into the sockets, how the eyelid folds over the eye and how one element of the face flows into another. Notice the contours, shapes and textures of each person you study. You will want to pay particular attention to the way the mouth is shaped, how the teeth fit into the jaw, and how the skin of the mouth delicately contours around the teeth.

Bodies come in three basic shapes, muscular, thin, and fat. Though the proportion rules apply to all three, the bodies appear completely different. They act differently too. When observing a heavy person, notice that they cannot put their arm straight down, it hangs out to the side at a forty five degree angle. It is also uncomfortable for heavy people to stand for any length of time with their feet together. On the other hand, thin people do not like to sit for very long, because their bones are so close to the surface that it actually hurts to sit.

Rules of thumb apply to limbs as well. The upper arm measures one head long from the armpit to the elbow. The lower arm extends one head long from the elbow to the wrist. The upper leg reaches two heads high from the crotch to the knee, while the lower leg hangs two heads long from the knee to the bottom of the foot. The hand equals the same length as the face from the chin to the bottom of the hairline, whereas the foot is the same height as the head. The illustrations define these generalities. There are of course exceptions, but following these general rules will help you properly proportion your doll. As the artist, you may on occasion alter the anatomy for special effects, but too much alteration disrupts realism.

A truly good sculptor learns to really see the human body and understand how it works and fits together. Notice how when the body bends from the waist the head stays centered over the feet. This prevents a person from falling over. When standing erect, our center of gravity is always over our feet. For a man to stick his right leg out to the side of his body, he must also put his left arm out equal distance and even move his body slightly to the left to compensate for the weight of his leg.

Have you ever noticed that the palm side of your fingers are twenty five percent shorter than the back side of your fingers? This is what I mean, learn to see the human anatomy. Notice wrinkles appear when one smiles, frowns or makes some other gesture with his face. When sculpting, only etch wrinkles in where they go naturally. Never do wrinkles for wrinkles sake, because there is a reason for each one. The same applies for lumps and bulges under the skin. Unless they are justified by muscle, fat or bone leave them out.

During my teaching seminars I encourage the students to carefully observe one another and even, with permission, touch one another to feel how the jaw fits into the skull, how the eyes fit into the sockets, or how the neck flows from the back of the head down to the shoulders. Study these thing before you start to sculpt. Once you learn to SEE people in this light you will notice things you never noticed before and you will also SEE the difference in your work.

CHAPTER 6
Sculpting the Head

SCULPTING THE HEAD

MATERIALS:

- 1 block of skin tone polymer clay
- 1 package of eyes (either a glass and plastic combination or all glass)
- One-half inch wooden dowel
- Medium weight aluminum foil
- Polyfill
- Sculpting tools
- Powdered brush-on makeup (skin tone and blusher)
- White, bisque, or light yellow clay for teeth (optional)
- Pink or rose colored clay for tongue (optional)
- Matte fixative - (spray can)

Sculpting the head is without a doubt the most important part of the doll. That is not to say that a beautiful head will alone make the doll, but it is an intricate part, the foundation upon which we build. The first thing most of us notice about a person is their head and how the features fit upon their face. These things are so impressionable that we usually judge age and character at a glance from the neck up. Consider the importance of these features as you prepare the armature for your doll's head. Have a clear image of what you wish to project.

To make the head the right size for your doll, there are a few basic generalizations you must follow. As mentioned in the fourth chapter, the average adult is seven to seven-and-one-half heads high. For the most realistic effects, you should plan to have seven heads equal the height of the doll. If sculpting a character doll, you may wish to vary somewhat, making your doll six heads high. For

demonstration within this text, I will refer to the scale of seven heads equals one body.

A head is generally only as good as the armature beneath it. Many artists have suggested different types of materials for armatures. After trying nearly all of them, I never found one better than good old-fashioned aluminum foil. Do not be tempted to try untested materials for your armature as it could be unsafe for both you and your sculpture. Some might suggest the use of polystyrene foam, (Styrofoam®, is a Dupont trademark for polystyrene foam), but I would especially caution against this. I have tested polystyrene foam eggs and have detected distortion due to melting and finally disintegration of the egg. Further, reports show that polystyrene foam gives off toxic fumes when heated to the melting point. I strongly recommend you stay with medium weight house-

hold aluminum foil as it is safe, inexpensive, readily available, long lasting, and molds easily to the shape of a human skull.

For the most realistic effect in a head, take a few moments to examine your own skull and those of others around you. Notice the contours and ridges. Let your hands get a good feel for what they will duplicate in foil. Use the following illustration as an additional aid. Here I have shown the basic shape of the head and named the surface bones.

This simple graphic illustration of the basic shape of the skull, along with your own sensitive touch, is generally all you need to shape your head armature. If you are an advanced student and wish an even more realistic skeleton, select a good anatomy book and work from that. You will find it helpful to learn the names of the bones in the body as we go along. That way, when I refer to the

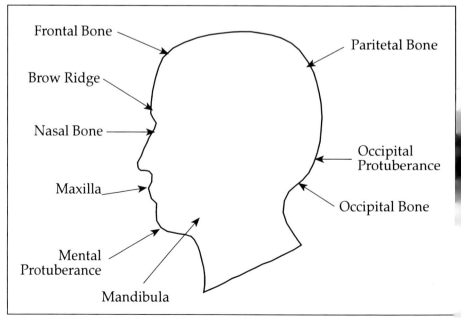

Head chart showing the major bones in the anatomy of the skull.

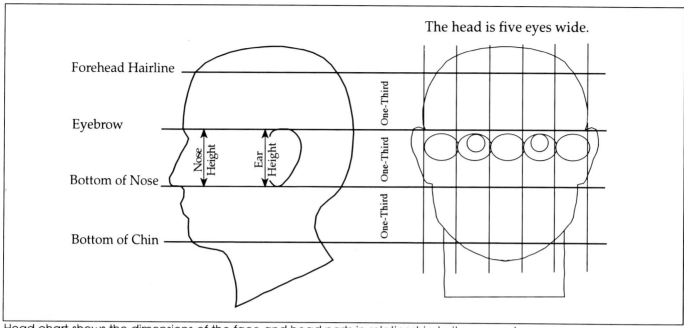

The head is five eyes wide.

Forehead Hairline

Eyebrow

Bottom of Nose

Bottom of Chin

Nose Height

Ear Height

One-Third

One-Third

One-Third

Head chart shows the dimensions of the face and head parts in relationship to its own parts.

occipital bone, for example, you will know that I am talking about the bump on the back of your head. Study the illustration to reinforce these terms.

To craft a three-inch high head armature, tear off a piece of foil about three feet long. To make a four inch head, use four feet of foil and roll it into an egg shaped ball as illustrated in the drawing. Make this egg soft enough so that you can sculpt the occipital lobe into the back of the head and the frontal bone at the front of the head. If sculpted too tightly, the head will not shape properly and you will need to start over. I like

to sculpt in the temples and the jaw structure at this time as well.

Make a second egg shape from front to back on the same armature to form the frontal lobe and the occipital lobe of the skull. This finished shape must look like a skull. If it does not, start over, and over, and over. Stay with it until you get it just right. Remember, once the clay is laid, you are committed to that shape. Work it until you are completely satisfied.

With the aluminum foil nicely shaped, make two platforms for the eyes in the middle third portion of the armature, by depressing a one-half inch dowel into set points on the armature. To determine where, follow this guide. The eyes should be one eye's width apart and one eye's width from each side of the head. As you see in the illustration, the head is five eyes wide. If your doll's head is 60mm's wide, you would want to use 12 mm eyes. If the head is as large as 120mm's wide, you may choose to use 24mm eyes.

If you want the eyes to look up or down, now is the time to make that adjustment in the aluminum armature. Press the wooden dowel

angling slightly up. This will cause the platform in the foil to angle up and when you place the eyes on the platform, they will also be looking up. Use the same method to make the eyes look down or off to the sides. After shaping the eye socket platforms, gently press the eyes into them.

Now you are ready to start laying the clay. Remember to first thoroughly knead your polymer clay for a minimum of ten minutes before using, as this helps eliminate troublesome air bubbles. Then make a ball of clay about one-and one-half inches high. Flatten the ball into a pancake one-fourth-inch

Hand-made three inch aluminum armature.

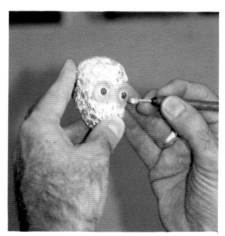

Head armature with eyes inserted.

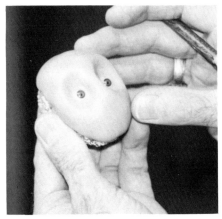
Head armature with face plate of clay and eyes inserted.

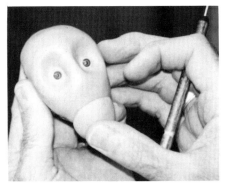
Head armature with face plate, eyes inserted and chin.

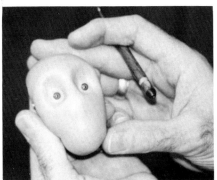
Head with face plate, eyes, and chin completely smoothed.

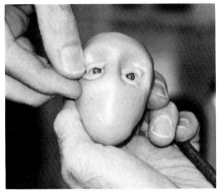
Placing eyelids on the face plate.

thick. Place the pancake over the face covering the eyes. Then lay your thumbs over the eye sockets to melt through the clay and expose the eyes. With your primary sculpting tool, push the excess clay back to expose the whites of the eyes.

Make another ball of clay about one-inch high and place it on the chin of the doll. Smooth it with your fingers and tools to see that it loses its joint line. Another small ball, about the size of a pea should be placed to form the end of the nose.

Roll two small pieces of clay for the upper and lower lips. As you see in the illustration, the width of the lips is the same width as the inside color of the eye. Smooth the rolls until they blend into the face plate. This is a very important step because sculpting the mouth helps form the character of the doll. Happiness, sadness, anger, and pain can all be expressed through the simple strokes of the sculpting tools. Notice in the photographs of my dolls, how even small changes can make great differences in the finished character of the face. Such changes in the lips can also determine age, sex, and even race. An old person has very thin lips, whereas a young child's lips are full. There are many different mouth shapes but only a few basic lip designs.

Experiment with the different variations and settle on the one that suits your doll's character best. Mold the clay into shape on the top and on the bottom lip until you are satisfied with the results. Remember, you are the master of

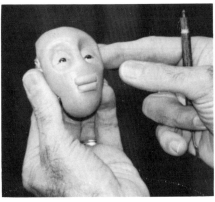
Eyelids in place with lips added.

the clay. Do not be afraid to push it around.

Next, we will form the eyelids by making two very small rolls. Place one at the top and one at the bottom of each eyeball. Smooth these rolls into top and bottom eyelids. With the eyes in place, we begin to sculpt the other facial features of the doll. Eye definition comes later in the sculpting process. Notice the progression shown in the photos. Smooth the

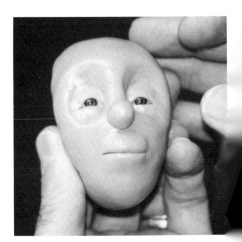
Nose placed on the face.

clay while adding many new details to support the character of the doll.

Form the nose by scoring down both sides of it and around the nose wings. Notice in the photo how I work the nose with my hands and tools until I have a shape I like. Consider the ancestry of your doll before shaping the nose. Example: The Roman nose is well known and very distinctive. Form your doll's nose accordingly.

While shaping the nose, you must also shape the philtrum or divot, the mound between the top lip and the bottom of the nose. This philtrum is made of cartilage and muscle. You may be able to form it by pushing the clay up from the lip, but if there is not enough clay, simply add more and sculpt it into place. We reshape the nose later during the sculpting process.

It is humorous to note that while most people wish for smaller noses for themselves, they tend to sculpt very large ones on their dolls. When this happens, I walk around class with the scissors snipping off the ends of many noses to a more realistic length. If you find that you too over extended, just snip it off and reshape.

Realism is sculpted into eyes by careful shaping of the lids above and below the eye. Bare in mind, that subtle changes to the lids can dramatically change the overall appearance of the doll. For example, the Betty Davis look can be achieved by keeping the lid to the upper eye tight against the eyeball, whereas a slack upper eyelid with fatty tissue above the eye offers the John Wayne look.

Shaping the lids also creates an array of moods; happy, sad, melancholy, worried or even angry. Experiment with the different looks as you sculpt the eyes and the tissue around them. You may

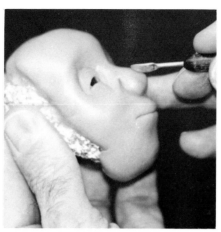

Smoothing the nose into place and scoring the nose.

find yourself changing the expression several times before you find a look you like.

The age and nationality or race can also be changed by altering the configuration of the eyes. All humans adapt to their surroundings, such things as color of skin, muscle development, hair color and the shape of their eyes change according to their environment. Notice the peculiarities when looking at different races and learn the differences. Once again I reinforce my favorite fundamental of sculpting, "Learn not just to look, but to see."

I once had a student in California unable to get the eyes right. She was so frustrated that she wanted to quit sculpting and I was just about ready to stop teaching. Then a thought struck. I carefully cut out a piece of an orange skin shaped like the oval of the eye. I held the orange up sideways and asked her to look at it. I showed her how, like the orange skin, the lid follows the contours of the eyeball. With that simple demonstration, the fog lifted from her mind. Within minutes she pro-

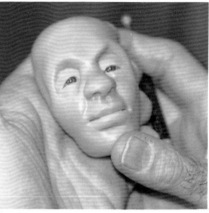

Basic elements in place and smoothed, ready to put on the finishing touches.

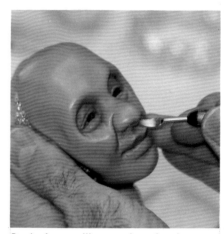

Basic face with powdered color added to wet clay.

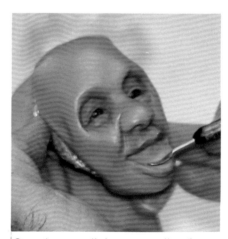

Opening mouth in preparation for teeth.

duced a pair of beautiful eyes. If you reach an impasse in eye making, take a break, cut into an orange to more clearly visualize the contours of the eye and lid. After accurately reproducing the shape of the lid, reward yourself.

Installing raw clay for teeth.

Shaping teeth and tongue.

Shaping the lips and adding detail.

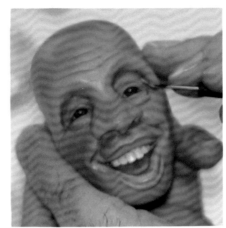
Adding detail to the eyes.

Take another break and enjoy the orange. You deserve it!

Teeth can be a tremendous asset to the sculpture. If you desire to add them, you may do so at any time as long as the clay is still wet. Use white, bisque, or light yellow clay for the teeth, depending on the age of your doll. Notice in the photos how the teeth look absolutely real. To place the teeth, open the doll's mouth as you would your own mouth to receive dental work. Open it slowly and carefully with your primary sculpting tool. If you pry the mouth open too fast, the corners will tear. Make a small bridge with the clay and insert it into the mouth. Separate the teeth with a scalpel knife. Roll the edges of the teeth with the primary sculpting tool. As you round the edges of each tooth, the gums will start to appear automatically. Flatten or round the bottom of the teeth depending on the age of the doll. You may now adjust the teeth to look even better by making one tooth crooked, chipped, or even remove it altogether. Remember, teeth are as much a part of the character of the doll as any other major part of the face.

Placing a tongue in after the top teeth are done adds realism. You can actually make it look as though the tongue is pressed against the teeth. Use pink or rose colored clay mixed with flesh color for the tongue. After placing it in the mouth, add the bottom teeth and carefully shut the mouth around the teeth. With all the major elements of the face in place, begin shaping the forehead, cheeks and chin. Notice in the photographs that I shape these with my thumbs and fingers, using the tools when needed for additional details. Do not put in character lines yet. These come after we apply the makeup.

To cover the entire head with a flesh colored patina, we apply a very light wash of makeup, china paint powder, or even chalk. All work well so choose your favorite. The colors depend on your tastes and the type of doll you are creating. There are many different colors on the market for you to choose from under various name brands. Just be certain the ones you buy are matte. Be aware that makeup applied to the wet clay shows up quite dark but lightens during the curing process by about fifty percent. While the clay is still wet, use a soft broad brush to apply the powders. Be careful not to get any powder in the eyes. Now wipe the residual powder off with your fingers. This leaves a natural oil on the surface of the clay.

If you ever use the wrong powder on the doll or otherwise make a mistake and need to take the powder off, you may do so by carefully wiping the sculpture with a soft cloth dampened with lacque thinner. Be very careful as the thinner does eat away at the top layer of the clay. Using it incorrectly will result in the ruin of your doll.

Begin adding color now, by first applying a light brown color around the eyes, nose and mouth with a soft brush about three eighth of an inch wide. Use light strokes. If your doll is male, you may want to add some of this dark color to his beard as well. Next put a rose color on the cheeks and forehead. If your doll is other than white Caucasian, choose a color of the same hue and family of color, then work in darker or lighter colors for accent.

With the color in place, you can begin to draw in the character wrinkles and facial texture. Remember, character lines are never added just for lines sake. Character lines are there because of years of repeating the same facial gestures. For example, if a person smiles a lot, that person will have smile lines. If he or she frowns frequently, then there will be frown lines. You can tell a great deal about a person's life by looking at the lines on their face. If a person has deep brow lines, you can bet they worry far too much. Deep lines around the eyes express too much time in the sun or suggest that the person suffers from impaired vision. To better understand the character lines of a face, observe others carefully or study your own face in the mirror. Wrinkle up your face and see how the lines act when you smile, frown or grimace. Then proceed to show your doll's true character by delicately etching lines around the eyes and mouth. If needed, extend these character

Completed Cheyenne Indian.

lines to the cheeks, brow, and forehead. You will find that the lines etch easily now because the powder on the clay changes its texture.

Once I decided to sculpt an Indian Princess, but could not get it to look quite right. I had rubbed the skin as smooth as a baby's butt and shaped the cheekbones and forehead as good as they could be. Still, it was not the Princess I wanted. It just did not feel right. I became so frustrated that I thought of throwing it in the trash and starting all over. Instead, I decided to have some fun with it. I added character lines to the smooth face to transform her into an old woman and found that she looked more like an old man to me. Once I settled with that new image, the sculpture took off. The photo on page 37 displays the result—an Indian Warrior that turned out to be one of my favorite pieces.

You may add realism to the skin texture by gently touching the face of the doll with a piece of Velcro or a soft tooth brush. I rub the sculpture against my beard for a real skin-like texture. After texturizing the face, add a bit more color by brushing the powder over the textured skin. The powder fills the low spot with a nice effect.

Your doll's face is now ready to be cured. Make sure to preheat and test the temperature of your oven before you put in your sculpture. All ovens vary in temperature

from day to day depending on the humidity of that day. After heating for several hours, most controls are not reliable. Therefore, get in the habit of always testing the oven with an oven thermometer every time you use it.

Make a polyfill nest in a small bowl to hold your piece. This will keep the face from touching the racks in the oven and distorting the clay. Place the sculpture face up in the bowl. Place the bowl in the middle of the oven, a good distance from any coils. Proceed to cure it at 250° for ten to fifteen minutes, venting for air, etc. Make sure the oven is at exactly 250°. A hotter temperature will burn the head. A cooler one will not completely cure. I have actually seen clay catch on fire from an oven that is too hot. If you need to cure at a temperature higher than 225°, do not use plastic eyes. The half glass/half plastic eyes work well up to 250°, but start to melt at temperatures above that. I recommend glass eyes for any sculpture cured above 250°. I have tested curing clay at 275° as recommended by some clay manufacturers

and do not suggest it. It is far too easy to scorch the head at that temperature. I recommend that you test a small portion of clay in your oven before curing the finished head.

You will know the head is properly cured if after ten minutes the skin looks matte. A shiny surface usually indicates undercuring. Sometimes a piece straight from the oven may still feel soft to the touch. This does not necessarily mean the sculpture is not done. Give it a chance to cool before testing it for hardness. The best cured pieces will be so hard that your fingernail could not scar them. If your piece fails this test, put it back in for another ten minutes. Extra time in the oven will not harm the clay. My own experiments prove that a piece left in the oven for hours does fine as long as the oven temperature is *not too high.*

There are times, when despite our best kneading and smoothing efforts, an air bubble escapes detection. During the curing process the air heats and expands, creating an even larger bubble of air under the clay. If this happens, DO NOT THROW THE HEAD AWAY. Leave it alone and let it cool. Then carve off the bump with your X-Acto knife. You will notice a large hole under the skin of the doll. Fill this hole in with clay and re-cure the head. After it is cured and cooled again, you can sand the edges of the new clay and rub the sanded area with lacquer thinner to restore this area to its original look.

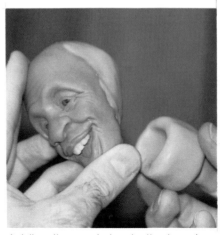

Adding the back of the head to the fired head.

Adding the neck ring to the head.

After curing the face, and allowing the head to cool, apply the back of the head by making a pancake about the same size of a cherry tomato. Flatten this into a pancake about 1/4 of an inch thick. Smooth the pancake on the back of the armature as you did the front and blend it with the hardened face plate. You may feather the wet clay over the hard clay. Then use the same makeup to color the wet clay as you used for the facial color. Notice that the cured clay is about 20% darker than the wet clay. Always take this into consideration when coloring the wet clay. Place the head in the oven face down in the nest of polyfill and cure for ten minutes at 250°.

To sculpt the neck, begin with a ball of clay about the size of a plum. Make that into a roll and then seam it together as in the photograph on page 38. Place the neck on the head and feather to blend. After sculpting the neck to the shape you like, add a little color to match the face. With the color placed, add detail in the neck with a needle tool. Cure the completed head 250° for ten minutes. Rest the head in the nest of polyfill with the wet clay up, so the heat and the weight of the head does not distort the wet clay.

After the head cools, but while it is still warm to the touch, place the ear on the doll. A few generalities will assist you in sculpting the ears. The ears are the same size as the nose, with the ear hole in the exact center of the head, with the flower of the ear in the back one-half. As you see in the photos, the ear requires a lot of detail so spend some time with it. Use the smooth

Smoothing, shaping and texturing the neck.

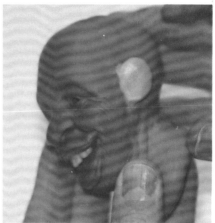

Adding the ear with raw clay to the fired head.

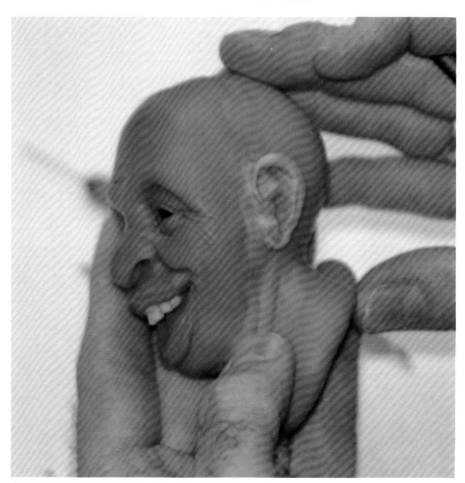

Sculpting the ear and adding the finishing color

ended lacing tool which I refer to as the ear tool.

Begin with a small ball of clay, about the size of a pea. Flatten this ball into the shape of an ear and place it on the head. Do not be tempted to sculpt your ears on the table, as you will not be able to transfer them from the table to the head without ruining them. Notice in the photographs on page 39, how I make the ear the same size as the distance between the eyebrow and the bottom of the nose. With the ears in place, sculpt a question mark into the ear. Also sculpt in the helix line and the antihelix, these are the two ridges that incircle the ear (look in the mirror or at a model for reference). Now sculpt in the ear canal and the earlobe. If you are having questions about the shape of the ear, ask someone to pose for you while you sculpt. The second ear may be sculpted to a perfect match by holding the first ear toward a mirror.

Once the ears are sculpted, you may fire them at the same temperature and time we have fired the other components. Set the cured head aside. Further painting and detailing of the face will be done in chapter nine.

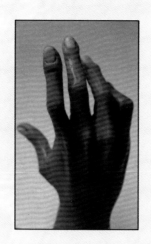

CHAPTER 7

Sculpting the Hands

SCULPTING THE HANDS

MATERIALS:
- Cernit
- Sculpting Tools
- 16 Gauge Brass Wire
- 24 Gauge Brass Wire
- Needle-nose Pliers
- White Floral Tape
- Hemostat or Vice Grips
- Needle Tool
- Convex Curved Utility Knife

The mere mention of hand sculpting strikes a cord of horror with most artists and may even cause some to break out in a cold sweat. I felt the same way when I started making dolls. That's why my first few Father Christmas pieces all wore gloved hands. I buried my head in the snow and put off learning to make them. However, I soon realized that to continue making dolls, I must lift my mind out of the deep freeze and learn to sculpt bare hands, no matter how unnerving the process. That's when I really began to understand the true horror of sculpting hands. But after much trial and error, I also came to understand that hands are difficult only if you allow them to be. When you remove the barriers to learning and receive proper instruction, hands become easier. In fact, through my simple techniques, not only will you not break out in a cold sweat, you might be surprised to find that you actually enjoy sculpting hands. I do not allow any Santa Claus dolls with mittens, gloved lady dolls, Captain Hooks, or dolls with their hands glued into their pockets, at least not until you learn how to make two good hands with your own

two hands. We make our hands from scratch in all my seminars and you should too.

My original hands, made without armatures, looked pretty good for a first attempt but did not hold up long enough to reach the collectors' home. Obviously, I guaranteed the workmanship and as a result re-made most of the original hands. That experience reinforced in my mind the importance of using a hand armature. It not only gives a platform to build the clay on, but adds tremendous strength to the finished hand. Even if a finger is broken, it will not fall off with an armature in place. Although ready-made hand armatures are available and may assist you when doing large editions, I do not recommend them for now. We will construct our own.

Experimenting and learning to develop my hand making technique proved arduous, but the results improved both the appearance and durablility of my pieces dramatically. In this chapter I will share the techniques that work for me, along with a few shortcuts I discovered on the road to sculpting realistic looking hands. So, shed your inhibitions and get ready for a great learning experience.

The human hand is divided into five phalanges (finger bones), four are connected by muscle, tendons, joints and skin. The other phalanx, the thumb is only connected to the others at the wrist. The four fingers have 180° of backward and forward movement, while the thumb can pivot a full 360°. This allows the thumb to touch any of the other fingers in the process of picking up objects or grasping things. As this is the natural way a

human hand is constructed, we will design our armature in much the same manner.

When sculpting the hand, you need to understand a few generalities concerning its dimensions. For example, the hand is the same length as an adult person's face, from the bottom of the chin to the top of the face at the hairline. With the fingers relaxed, the width of the hand from the tip of the thumb to the tip of the little finger, is the same as the length. With them extended, you can draw a circle around the hand and all fingers come to the edge of the circle. The palm is the same width as it is high. The middle finger, is generally the same length as the palm of the hand. The palm side of the finger is twenty-five percent shorter than the front side, due to the pad covering the knuckles inside the hand. The best model for creating hands is your own hand. As we have a tendency to make dolls that look like us to begin with, we might as well do so with our hands. Just as we have bones, muscles, and tendons holding our fingers together, so will we design

Photo of hand armature with wrist wrapped with 16 guage wire.

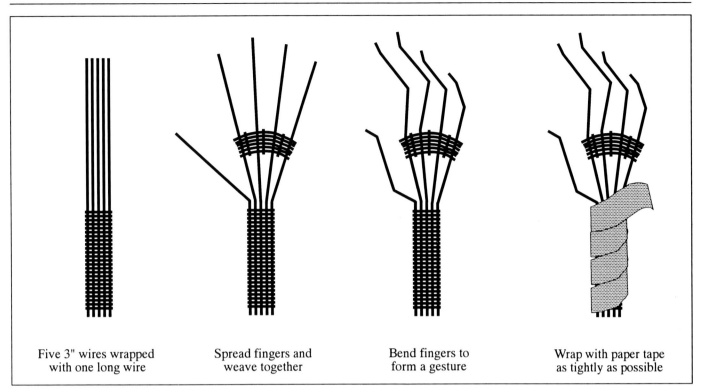

| Five 3" wires wrapped with one long wire | Spread fingers and weave together | Bend fingers to form a gesture | Wrap with paper tape as tightly as possible |

the armature. Begin by tying five 16 gauge wire phalanges together with a strand of 24 gauge wire. Notice the wire is wrapped around the wrist of the hand to strengthen the hand and to hold the base of the phalanges together.

Wrist wrapped, knuckles wrapped with 24 guage wire.

Spread the fingers into a fan hape. Weave 24 gauge wire around the four phalanges to form he understructure for the knuck-es. In each case as we wrap the wire, we must make it tight, thus helping to hold the fingers into their respective positions. Wrap only the four fingers together; the thumb will be attached at the wrist. If the wrapped wire should slip off, cut another piece of wire and begin the wrapping process again. This is faster and easier than trying to realign it.

After wrapping the fingers with wire, cut them to the desired length, using your own hand as the proportional guide. Measure the doll's hand by holding the armature up to the face of the doll and seeing that the base of the palm is to the bottom of the chin and the middle finger is to the bridge of the nose. The armature is naturally smaller than the finished hand will be because the clay goes over the top of the armature. Notice the four fingers are wrapped together, with the thumb being wrapped only to the wrist. This is just like the human hand; the fingers are attached to one another, but the thumb is separated, thus adding to its ability to pinch against the other fingers and provide 360° of mobility.

Once the fingers are cut to the proper length, you will bend them into the shape you desire. Bending the wire is done with a pair of needle-nose pliers. Only bend the first two knuckles of each finger. Later, when you add the clay, you may sculpt in the third knuckle. If you bend the third knuckle into the armature, the hand will look too much like a claw and you will not be pleased.

With the fingers wired together and bent to meet the gesture of the doll, you can shape the fingers to perform some set function. For example, if you want them to hold a bottle or some other accessory, now is the time to bend the wire around the accessory. Once you add the clay to the hand, the fingers will be thicker, so you must allow for that extra bulk.

Now wrap the armature with floral tape. I suggest using white floral tape, as it does not show through the clay like dark tape and there is no stain associated with its use. The purpose of the tape is to keep the clay from slipping on the wire armature and to add body to

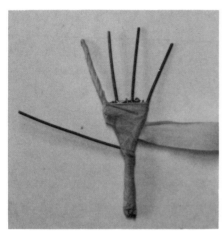

Wrapping the hands with paper tape.

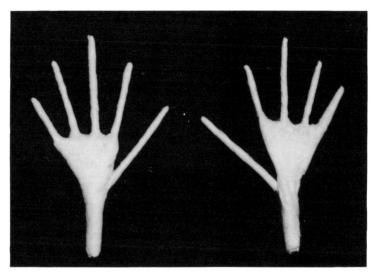

Hands wrapped with paper tape.

the hand before applying the clay. Wrapping the tape around the wire is done just like wrapping a bandage around a human hand or foot. Let the tape hold itself in place. Wrap a generous amount of tape around each finger, palm and wrist until the armature starts to look like a hand. As you stretch the paper tape, it activates the wax adhesive so it sticks together.

To help hold the armature while applying the clay, use a pair of hemostats or vise grips tightly fastened to the lower wrist. Make strips of clay and wrap them around the armature just like you did the floral tape. Keep the thickness of the clay consistent and just thick enough to put a skin texture over the wire and tape armature. As you apply the clay, the hand starts to look real. At this point, you must add additional clay for muscles and knuckles. Do not be tempted to make arthritic hands just because they may look like

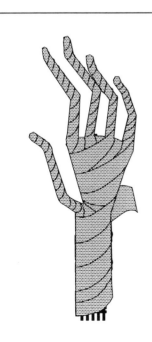

Wrap the entire hand as tightly as possible

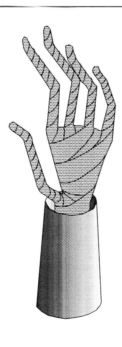

Cover hand with clay

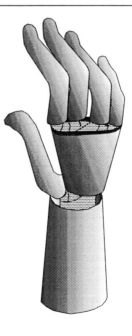

Wrap each finger, palm, back of hand, and wrist

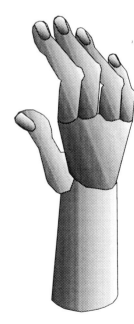

Blend all of the clay together and detail

that in the beginning. Continue to refine the hands until they look realistic. Add such detail as creases in the knuckles, slight indications of bones and even blood vessels.

The fingernails are achieved by scoring the outline of the finger nail with a needle tool. You should also make a line under the end of the nail with a scalpel or very sharp knife. After you have scored the nail, give it dimension by shaping it with your sculpting tool. You can make the nail so realistic that you can actually file the nail when you are done. Add the finishing touches like wrinkles and veins. Veins will push up automatically as you work the clay down on each side of them. Do not make the veins too prominent, just prominent enough to be seen. The same is said for knuckles, wrinkles, muscles and bone structure.

Firing the hands should be done at 250° for ten to twenty minutes, depending on the size and thickness of the hands. The hands can be cured longer at a higher temperature (260°) than the head because they have no eyes to worry about melting. It is best to leave the hemostats attached to the hands while they are curing; this will provide you with a base to hold the hands upright in the oven and prevent them from falling over and becoming damaged. You may want to put them in a nest of polyfill in case the sculpture should fall over. Be sure to use an oven mitt when removing the hemostats as they do get quite hot and can cause a nasty burn.

After the hands are cured and cooled, you will remove the hemostats to add the wrist or arm. If the

Starting to cover armature with clay.

Make a donut to cover palm.

Make a pancake to cover the back of the hand.

Make a wristband.

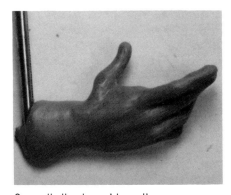
Smooth the hand together.

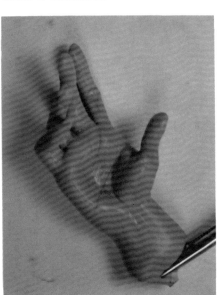
Shows underside of finished hand.

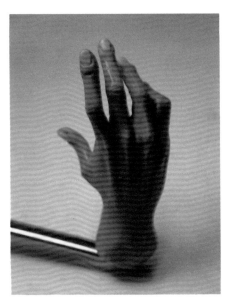
Shows front side of finished hand.

hemostats become embedded in the hardened clay, carefully carve away the excess clay with the scalpel pointing away from you. Cut off any unwanted clay and add the wrist by rolling a small piece of clay. As long as you add the wrist at a natural seam line or fold in the skin, you will not see where it attaches. Add shadowing or skin tone blush powder to help blend if desired and sculpt in wrist lines or veins and tendons as appropriate, then oven cure the wrist as you did the hand.

Once you have fired the hand and the wrist you may paint for further realism. Painting the hands is great fun as it brings them to life. Facial make-up powder and acrylic paints seem to work the best for me, however, you can use oil paints as well. I like to paint shadows, age spots, the white in fingernails, blood vessels and sometimes even hair. You can put as much detail into the hands as you desire, generally the more the better. However, beginning students may wish to keep it fairly basic until their skill level improves. Remember, well-crafted hands not only bring life to a doll, they help tell its life story. You must build as much character into the hands as possible.

The accompanying photographs show a pair of hands in their completed state before mounting them to the body. Notice these hands only extend to the forearm of a doll dressed in long sleeves. If you wish to dress a doll in short sleeves, you will make your wire armature the full length of the arm and complete the arm in the second firing just as you did the wrist and forearm.

With your first hand completed, begin the identical process over again to sculpt your second hand. Make certain that you have one hand for each side of the body. You might think this a fairly obvious point to mention, and I would agree, except that invariably at least one student in every sculpting class makes two hands that fit the same side of the body. During one particular seminar, working with an attentive group of students, I thought we might not encounter the problem. Then four hours later a student let out the all

too familiar, 'Oh, No!' Sure enough, she sculpted two left hands and had to bear the nick name Lefty for the duration of the seminar. It makes for a good laugh, but causes the artist much frustration. The only thing a student in that situation can do is hope someone else made two right hands. Then we just exchange hands and everyone leaves a happy camper. Otherwise, the artist must begin all over again making a third hand, hopefully the right one this time. You can avoid much aggravation by carefully scrutinizing your first hand before beginning the second.

Congratulations! You just sculpted your own pair of hands from scratch. With practice, you will become an old "hand" at it.

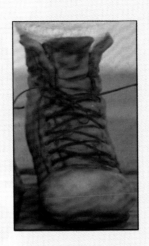

CHAPTER 8

Sculpting Feet & Shoes

SCULPTING FEET & SHOES

MATERIALS:
- Aluminum Foil
- Kemper 23 cleaning tool and lacing tool
- X-Acto knife, with convex blade
- White floral paper tape
- Polymer clay - 500 grams (Cernit, Fimo, Sculpey, etc.)
- Acrylic paint - brown, white, black or other desired color
- Lacquer thinner
- Quilting thread or dental floss
- Tubular gauze
- Sanding pad or varying grades of sandpaper
- Clear lacquer gloss paint

Before you go another step fur-ther, you need to determine whether your particular doll would look best barefooted or dressed in shoes crafted to complement the costume. Many sculptors opt for the barefooted look simply because it eliminates the nearly impossible search for a pair of in scale, realistic looking shoes to match their unique doll. Often, try-ing to locate such shoes turns into a task of nightmarish proportions, due to the fact that there are very few specialized shoe companies crafting shoes for one-of-a-kind dolls. After what seems like an endless search, dollmakers may try to adapt a pair of manufactured baby doll shoes for their one-of-a-kind golfer, bag lady, Santa Claus or teenager, only to discover that it never seems to look quite right. In despair, they settle for less than perfect shoes on their prized dolls, or simply go without any at all.

If you have ever faced this dilemma, you are going to love the solutions I offer in this chapter.

They will help you handcraft all your own doll shoes. I reveal sim-ple techniques that are less time consuming, less frustrating, less expensive, and a whole lot more fun than attempting to find the right ready-made shoes. These nonremovable shoes are construct-ed of clay and built right over the top of the fired foot. Where bare feet are appropriate to create an effect, by all means use them. The armature for bare feet and those with shoes is identical. The tech-nique for forming the toes is much like that of sculpting the hands. To become a truly well-rounded artist, both methods must be learned and mastered.

If you choose to construct custom-made shoes, you will enjoy the tremendous sense of pride that comes from knowing that you did the job yourself. Your doll will actually be worth more, since collectors tend to place a higher value on art dolls crafted entirely by the artist.

I strongly recommend a field trip to properly learn to make shoes. Take a few hours off to visit a cobbler's shop. If you do not have one in your area, go to a shoe repair shop. Ask the cobbler to show you the simple steps in-volved in shoe construction. The methods are exactly the same as those used in making shoes for polymer dolls, with the exception that we use glue instead of stitch-ing. Become familiar with trade terms such as the vamp, counter, upper, and other obscure names. Remember, this is a trade as old as shoes themselves. I enjoyed my visit tremendously and came away enlightened and inspired.

The first step is to construct an

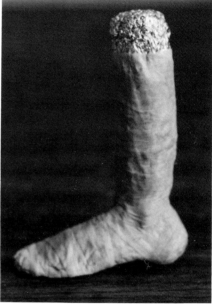

Foot armature wrapped and ready for clay.

armature for the foot and lower leg. This is done from one square foot (12 inches x 12 inches) of alu-minum foil. Softly roll and crum-ple the foil into a tubular shape about the size of a cigar. It should not be crumpled too hard—leave some body in it. If your doll's head is 3 inches high from the chin to the top of the head, your fin-ished foot will be 3 inches too. Bend the roll at a point 2 1/2 inches from the toe to make the heel (remember the armature will appear smaller than the finished foot after the clay is added). Now, bend the foil above the foot 3 inches to make the knee. The excess foil that is bent down from the knee will serve as the bulk for the calf muscle and back of the leg. By compressing the foil with your hands, soft sculpt the foil to the exact form of an actual foot and leg. Use your own leg and foot as live models. Cover the alu-minum armature with white paper

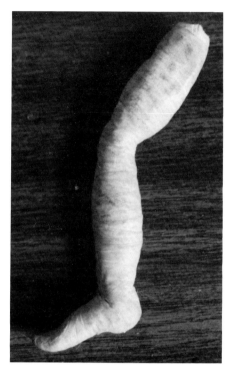

Leg armature wrapped and ready for clay

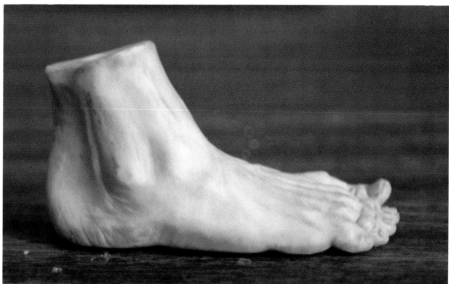

Completed foot

floral tape by wrapping the tape around the armature until it is completely encased. Sculpting may be done even as the tape is added by making more wraps around the calf and heel for example. Wrap the armature just as you would a broken ankle or a mummy. The more you wrap, the more shape you can put into the sculpture. After you have completed the leg and foot, you may manipulate the joints to fit any position. If you plan to create a runner or a doll who wears a high heeled boot, bend and shape the foot now to accommodate that type of shoe. The tape and aluminum foil will allow you to bend the limbs in any direction and as many times as you like while you are posing your doll. When you are satisfied with the shape and pose, you may proceed to the next step.

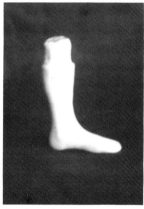

Foot sculpted over the top of an aluminum armature

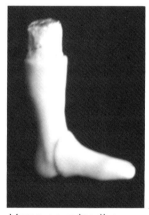

Vamp covering the front of the foot

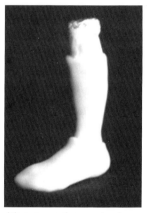

Vamp and counter in place

Make a role of clay about a foot long and flatten it out to resemble a half-inch wide belt. The clay should be about one-eighth inches thick. Wrap this clay around the armature just as you did the paper tape. Blend the clay with your fingers, making the basic shape of a smooth leg and foot. Do not neglect constructing a left and a right foot, and shape the arch accordingly.

If you plan bare feet, take the time now to sculpt toes into the

soft clay past the end of the armature. You need not build an armature inside the toes. Then add realistic details to the foot just as you did the hands in chapter seven, by raising up the knuckles, tendons and veins. Again, if you have difficulty, use your own bare foot as a model. After sculpting in the details, you may brush on flesh tone powdered makeup to the leg and foot as you did the hands, adding a touch of blush where needed. If you prefer shoes, you

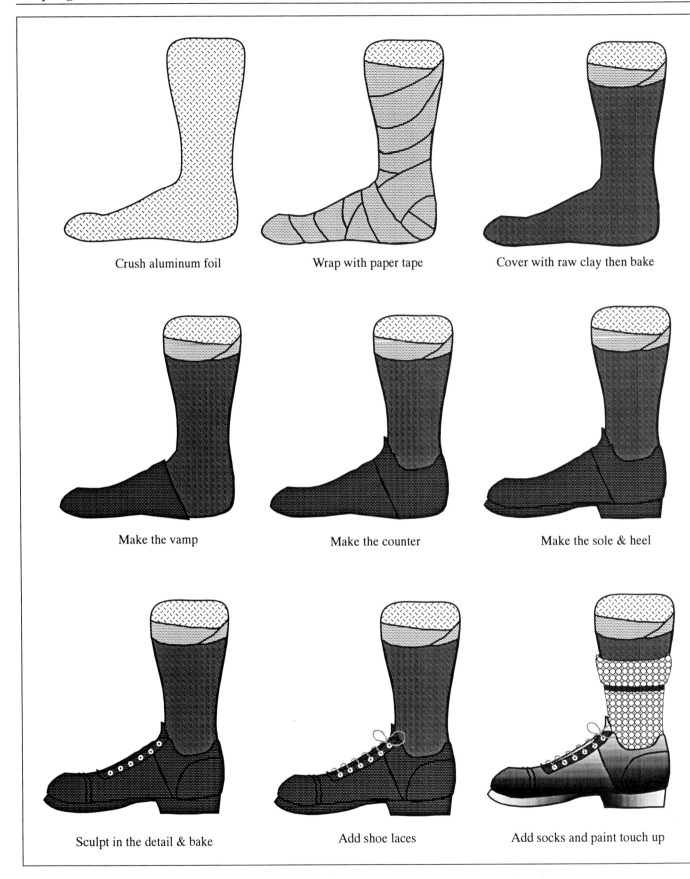

Crush aluminum foil

Wrap with paper tape

Cover with raw clay then bake

Make the vamp

Make the counter

Make the sole & heel

Sculpt in the detail & bake

Add shoe laces

Add socks and paint touch up

need not finish off the foot as the shoe is built over the basic shape of the foot eliminating the need to sculpt toes. Either way, bake the sculpture at 250˚ for 10-20 minutes.

When commissioned to sculpt Winston Churchill in his three piece suit and wing-tipped shoes,

was unable to find a realistic pair
of quarter scale shoes on the market. Making the shoes was my
only alternative. Since that experience, I have made shoes for my
Jazz Player, Jogger, Hiker,
Mountain Man, Cowboy, Soldier,
Mark Twain, Astronaut, and even a
Fisherman. When making shoes,
you are only limited by your time
and imagination. This chapter will
help you in handcrafting doll
shoes.

Shoes can be made out of
almost any medium, including
clay, leather, paper maché, or even
wood. I have chosen polymer clay
as the base for the shoe. Add-ons
to the polymer shoes may consist
of leather, thread, paint, fabric,
jewels, or metal buckles.

With the leg now hardened
(cured), cover the foot with a thin
layer of clay everywhere you want
the shoe to be. Cut off the excess
clay with the X-Acto blade and
smooth. A thin one-sixteenth of an
inch layer of clay should be evenly
placed over the shoe area of the
armature. Notice in the illustration
that once the clay is smooth, you
may sculpt seams as if the shoe
was sewn together. You may sculpt
any style of shoe you desire. The
sole is applied by making a thick
piece of clay and placing it on the
bottom of the foot. After placing
the thick flat sole on the bottom of
the shoe, cut the excess clay away,
just as you would if you were
making cookies with a cookie cut-
ter. With the sculpting tool, add
detail to the shoe. At this time, it
can be anything you want it to be,
from a slipper to a hiking boot.
They are all made the same way to
this point. For the purpose of this
book, I have chosen to finish the

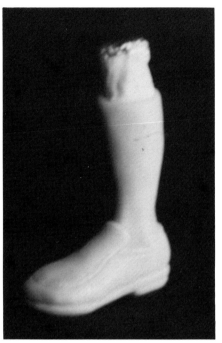
Sole and heel put into place.

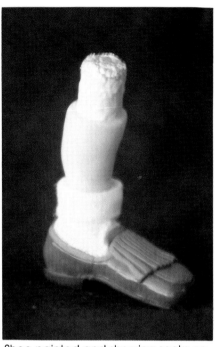
Shoe painted and showing socks on.

shoe as a stylish loafer.

Once the shoe has all of the
basics in place, you may choose to
sculpt holes in the shoe for laces
and glue quilting string or dental
floss into the holes to represent
shoelaces. Place and glue one end
of the string in the first hole.
Stretch the string to the next hole
and glue it down, then move on to
the next, just like lacing your own
shoes. Or you may follow a similar process for drilling holes and
lacing the shoes after the curing.
For more details you may add a
miniature belt buckle, buttons and
even real leather straps, etc. to the
shoes. I have cut a flap with fringe
from a thin piece of clay and
attached it to the top of the loafer,
but it may just as easily be constructed from real leather and
baked right into the clay during the
curing process. Cure the shoe for
the same amount of time you did
the leg. After the shoe has com-

pletely cooled, about twenty minutes, cut away any unwanted clay
with a convex curved blade.
Consider sculpting in more detail
as you cut with the knife. Be careful not to attempt this while the
shoe is still hot as it will crack and
break.

After you finish sculpting with
the knife, sand the sculpted areas
to smooth out the knife cuts and
gently brush the shoe all over with
lacquer thinner using a small brush
or Q-tip. The lacquer thinner will
eat away any rough edges caused
by sanding or cutting. Now your
shoe is ready to garnish either with
paints or other accessories (if you
did not already do this before curing). Additional information on
finishing your cured polymer
shoes with paints and lacquer is
detailed later in chapter nine.

The experienced dollmaker will
even sculpt the shoe, fire it, and
then cover the completed shoe in

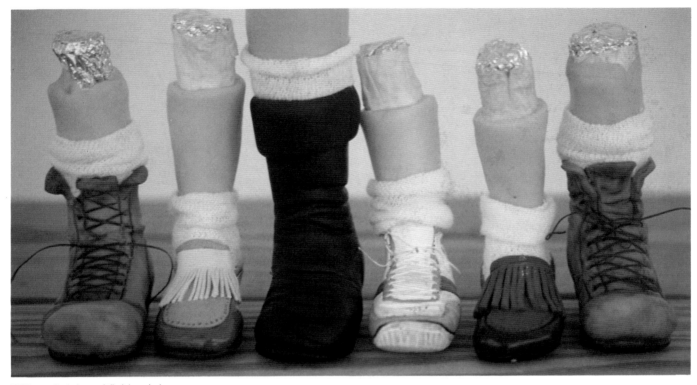

Different styles of finished shoes.

kid glove leather. This process is only for the skilled crafter, but it does make for a very realistic shoe. If you cover the entire shoe with leather, make sure the clay is smoothed so lumps do not appear under the leather as this seriously detracts from the realism. Glue the leather to the clay with a white glue such as Tacky or Elmer's. The best glue I have found when gluing leather is a glue called "Leather Weld™," sold by "Tandy Leather."

After laying the leather over the clay, wrap it around the bottom of the shoe and add a leather sole. The sole should be cut out of thick leather or you may use thin leather glued to a piece of thin cardboard. In any case, when using leather always hide the edges and corners of the leather by tucking them

underneath or into the deep seams of the clay.

The sock is made from tubular gauze, available at most pharmacies or medical supply houses. Cut a strip of gauze and slip it over the leg. Glue the bottom of the sock to the leg at the point where the shoe and leg meet. If white socks seem inappropriate, the gauze may be dyed with tea, coffee, or clothing dye. After the sock is glued in place, fold the sock down to complement the shoe design. I have sculpted several different pairs of shoes for this lesson, such as boots, tennis shoes and two pairs of loafers, one with leather fringe and the other with clay fringe. Additional tips on finishing your shoes with paints may be found in chapter nine.

Note that clay may also be put over the top of a fired porcelain leg and foot in the exact same manner used with the hardened polymer clay. You may put the porcelain leg in the oven to cure the clay. The clay will harden and the heat will not harm the porcelain. There is no shrinking to polymer clay during the curing process.

Now that you know how to make your own shoes, you will never have to rely on converting baby doll shoes to fit your one-of-a-kind doll again. Exhibit your doll with pride, show off your handcrafted shoes, and always put your best foot forward!

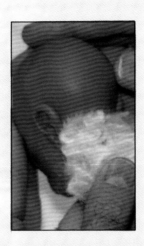

CHAPTER 9

Finishing the Head, Hands & Feet

MATERIALS:

- Sanding pads or paper of varying grades
- Lacquer thinner or acetone
- Clear fingernail polish
- Nylon stocking
- Soft cotton cloth
- Matte spray fixative
- Gloss spray fixative
- Acrylic paints (colors optional)
- Soft paint brushes both broad and thin
- Shoe accessories as desired
- Hot glue gun
- Ready-made mohair wig or natural mohair braids
- Scissors

Face

Face painting is the most thrilling part of dollmaking for many artists, including myself. In those final moments of painting we gently stroke the doll to life. The change is chilling. Suddenly, your doll transforms from a lifeless lump of clay, to a life-long friend who bares testimony to your skill as a dollmaker. Most artists feel so attached to their first doll that they never give it up. Those who do part with them eventually regret it. I remember well the feeling of finishing my first doll. As crude as it was, after painting in those final facial details, it sprang to life before my eyes. I felt as though a piece of myself went into that new creation. Before the final painting of the facial features, the head surface must first be prepared. Those with perfectly smooth sculptures may skip this step and proceed to the actual painting process. If your head needs work, however, begin now

to erase seam lines and carve away unwanted bumps until you have a perfectly smooth head. This is also your last chance to sand and patch any leftover creases or ridges caused by air bubble repairs. For this smoothing process you will need either sanding pads (made for sanding greenware) or a package of varying grades of sandpaper, lacquer thinner or acetone and a broad brush. I do not recommend sanding on the face of the doll. Even though you may be able to achieve a very smooth texture by using different grades of sanding pads, you will never get the surface back to it's original appearance. I sand only the top of the head and the neck when I smooth a doll.

Sanding proves cleaner and more effective if done under water. This not only keeps the polymer dust down, which some people may be allergic to, it also keeps the dust from collecting in the crevices of the doll's head. Sanding polymer clay opens minute air holes in the clay. When you open these holes, the sanding powder fills them and leaves little white marks on the surface. Sanding under water helps to eliminate these white pits. Always sand in circular motion and be careful not to put undue pressure on the ears or nose as they may break off. Begin sanding the head with coarse paper and work your way to a lighter grit while continuing to smooth the surface. After sanding to your satisfaction, you may restore the original surface and remove sanding lines by painting with lacquer thinner or acetone (the fumes from these solvents may be toxic, so please use only in

well-ventilated areas). The solvents work by actually eating away the top surface of the clay which then removes all scratch marks. If you get lacquer thinner on the plastic eyes of the doll, it will substantially dim their luster. After final painting of the eye and application of lashes, the luster may be restored to the eye, by simply applying a coat of clear fingernail polish to the eyeball area.

Once you have sanded the head and painted it with lacquer thinner, you may highly polish it with a nylon stocking and then buff it with a cotton tee-shirt. You may also buff the face to look like wax over porcelain if you desire. I personally prefer a matte finish on the faces of my dolls.

With the head thoroughly cured smoothed and polished, you are now ready to complete the painting of the facial features. If you have never painted on cured polymer clay before, you may want to experiment first on a cured piece of clay until you develop a feel for it because painting the cured head with acrylic paint is somewhat different than painting with facial powder and china paint that we used in chapter six. The powders give a very natural color to the cheeks, forehead, and around the shadow of the eyes but you will have to use acrylic paint to make hard lines of paint. I personally prefer acrylic paints for the sharp detail and in addition to china paint and ladies' makeup for larger areas. I use Grumbacher acrylic paint, however, there are many different manufacturers for you to choose from. Just be sure to test the paint on cured clay first. The colors used for painting the head

and hands are as follows:
- Burnt Umber
- Raw Umber
- Cadmium White
- Crimson Red
- Colonial Blue

If you prefer not to mix your own colors, premixed colors are available. Either way, you will notice that the color does not go on as easily when the clay is hard as it did when soft. To overcome this, you may spray a very light coat of matte fixative over the face. I strongly caution against a gloss spray as it will ruin the doll. When spraying the fixative, hold the can about 12 inches away from the object. In a sweeping motion, start spraying before you get to the object and continue to spray until you have passed the object. By keeping this motion as you spray, you will never make a puddle on the surface. Nothing will ruin a doll faster than paddling the spray on the surface. Never spray directly at the subject, always use the broad sweeping motion. It is critical that you follow these directions for spraying. After painting the entire face, we use fixative once again to seal the paint and make-up.

First, line the eyes under the upper eyelids with a dark brown acrylic paint to define the eye, add depth, and give the appearance of eyelashes. You may additionally choose to paint in eyelashes or use real ones. For a beautiful lady doll or child, I recommend real eyelashes, applied later. These should be baby lashes with waxed bottoms, available at most studios or doll shops. For an older character, stay with the dark line under the upper lid as described.

Additional makeup may be added around the eyes for shadow and character. Apply much like a lady puts on eye shadow. The color to be used for this will vary from purple to gray or even brown, depending on what you have in mind for your design. When painting in the shadows, make sure to blend the paint lightly with several coats until you have it dark enough.

There is an unwritten rule that applies when painting a doll's head, "less is more." The best way to master this is to always paint with very low pigment washes (a lot of water). Let each coat thoroughly dry before applying the next coat. The same is true when using powders, start light and work up to darker colors. I paint with acrylics, china paints, and powdered makeup all on the same head. I even confess to using magic markers and pencil. As far as I'm concerned, if it achieves the effect you want, use it. Just remember to always fix the colors with a matte spray fixative.

After painting the eyelids you may now paint the outer lining of the eyeball (eyeball, not eyelid) with red paint. To paint the outer ridge of the eyeball use a very small wet brush to lay paint between the eye and the eyelid. Let the capillary action of the wet paint naturally flow around the eye. If you get too much paint around the ridge of the eye, use a clean wet brush to remove the excess paint. You will be able to remove as much as you like as long as the paint is wet. Once the paint is dry, it is there to stay.

If you choose to apply real lashes, do so now by cutting them into small sections and pressing them right to the eyeball, under the upper lid. With the lashes stuck into place, paint the eyeball with fingernail polish. The polish will restore luster to the eye and hold the lashes into place like glue.

You may wish to paint the lips with acrylic paint to achieve a sharp line on the lip. This should be done with colors ranging from light peach to dark crimson. Use a very wet brush (lots of water and very little pigment); this gives the paint a translucent look just right for lips. After the paint dries—about two minutes—paint a second coat or more as needed to achieve the depth and intensity of color which you desire. You may also use a touch of powder over the paint to soften the look. In other words, work it until it looks right to you then spray with a light mist of fixative to seal the powder and paint.

If rose colored clay was not used to construct the tongue, you may achieve a more realistic tongue by painting it a darker hue of the same color used to paint the lips. The teeth may be painted with a very light patina of gray mixed with a very light yellow, depending on the age and character of the doll. If sculpting a child, stay with the natural white clay. If bisque or off-white were used to sculpt the teeth of an older character, you need not paint them.

Add color to the cheeks and nose for a more ruddy complexion. Feather the color in with a soft brush. Very light dabs of paint around the nose and cheeks works for freckles or age spots. I prefer to paint the spots on and then blot them out with my finger. This

Unpainted face.

Painted face.

causes them to diffuse and look much more natural. Added lines also highlight the wrinkles.

Hands and Bare Feet

Painting the hands and feet is done with the same acrylic colors, makeup or china paint used for the head. After painting the patina over the entire hand, you will paint the fingernails with a very light

Completed hand.

coat of darker flesh colored pigment, then paint the tips of the fingernails with ivory or off white to represent the extended part of the nail and even the moon shape at the base of the nail. Look to your own nails for realism.

If the hand you have made shows veins, you may paint them with a very light blue wash (Colonial Blue). This blue wash should be so light that it only appears to be blue but is not overbearing. As with the head, you may wish to add aging spots to the hands by dabbing them on with a brush and blotting them with your fingertips. The same blue may be used on the veins in the foot and even on the temples of an older person. Here too, you may wish to work from a photograph or a live model to assure more realistic veins. I do not recommend bulging veins on a small child or a beautiful lady doll.

Shoes

Your polymer shoes may be finished in several ways. I prefer to paint my cured shoes with an opaque matte finish (opaque meaning solid color, very little water, almost pure pigment), thus giving them a look which more closely resembles natural leather. Make certain the paint you choose will dry on polymer clay; some do not. Then spray with matte fixative. You may also paint the shoes two-toned as with saddle shoes or even paint in stitching or seam lines before adding the fixative.

Another method of painting your polymer shoes lends a patent leather look to them. This is achieved in the same manner as above, except that after applying the paint and allowing it to dry, you then apply several coats of gloss enamel fixative. If you sculpted your polymer shoes in

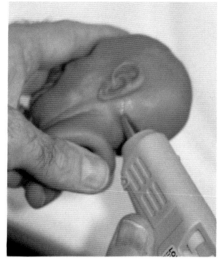

Applying glue strand

Finished shoe with laces and antiquing

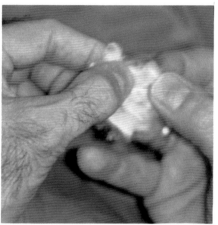

Stretching hair strand for application to head

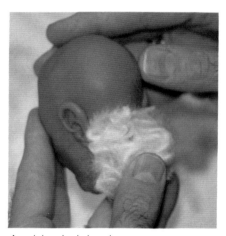

Applying hair to glue

colored clay and are happy with the results, but still seek the patent leather look, go ahead and apply the coats of gloss enamel fixative over your colored clay.

The third and last method for dressing up the paint is to add an antiqued look. This is achieved by first painting the shoe just as we did in method one. Then, when it is completely dry, brush-dry china paint or makeup powder into the low spots and seams of the shoe. Wipe off the excess powder and then spray with matte fixative to hold the leftover powder in place. This makes a wonderful old looking shoe.

An even more realistic look may be achieved by drilling holes in the clay shoes with a $1/16$ to $1/32$ inch drill bit where the shoe laces go, insert and glue very small brass grommets into the holes (the grommets are made as electrical plugs for miniature doll houses and can be purchased at most miniature shops). After the grommets are glued into place, glue

laces made of heavy thread, dental floss, buttonhole thread or even light yarn, into the holes. Let the glue in each hole dry before gluing the next. Lace the shoes up by gluing from hole to hole to the top, then tie into a bow. The shoes shown above are completely made of Cernit with cotton shoelaces. Let your imagination and creativity guide you for other little touches. If that fails, dig through your closet to find a pair of old shoes for a model.

Hair

The next thing that brings the doll to life is applying the hair. If you are making a child or beautiful lady, you may wish to buy a pre-made wig. If you are buying a wig I recommend mohair. The mohair wigs are of the right scale for these dolls. Natural hair wigs are too coarse for this scale, and acrylic wigs are cheap looking for one-of-a-kind dolls. When you pick out the mohair wig, you may be shocked at the price, but believe me, it will enhance your doll well beyond the expense of the wig.

If you are making an old lady,

man or character doll like Santa Claus, I recommend making the wig yourself which is not nearly as hard as it sounds. In fact, the process for this is really rather simple. Begin with natural mohair. It can be purchased in braids, open strands or wefted. Wefted means it is cleaned, combed and sewn together. This is the best of all mohair and is also the most expensive. I use the mohair braids for most of my dolls. It works very well for this type.

To begin with the braid, cut sixteen pieces of hair about $1\frac{1}{2}$ inches long. Spread the pieces as you see in the photograph to about 2 inches wide. Lay all of the pieces on the table. Choose the ones with the best shape or curl to

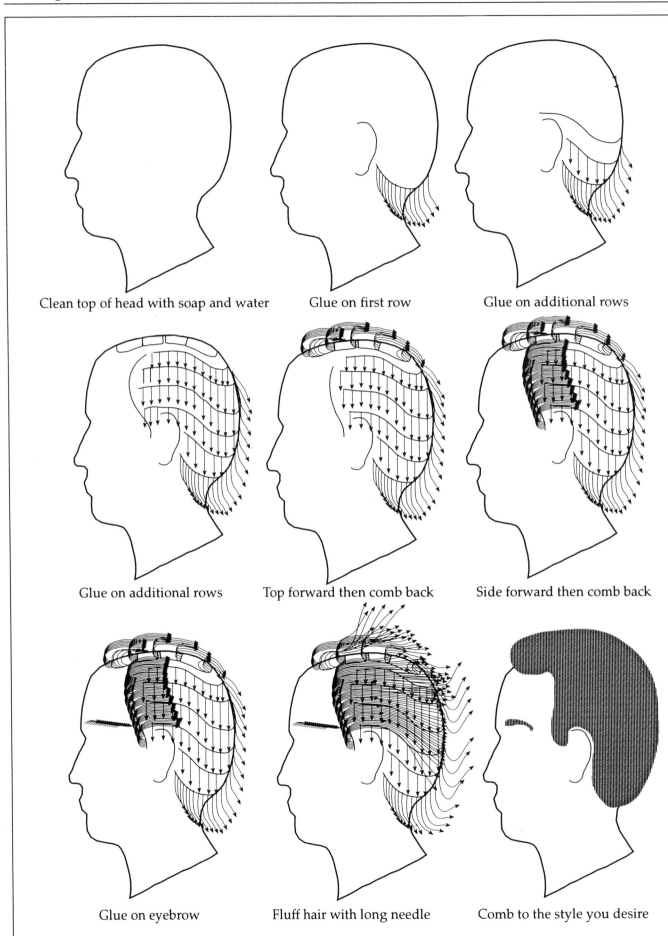

Clean top of head with soap and water

Glue on first row

Glue on additional rows

Glue on additional rows

Top forward then comb back

Side forward then comb back

Glue on eyebrow

Fluff hair with long needle

Comb to the style you desire

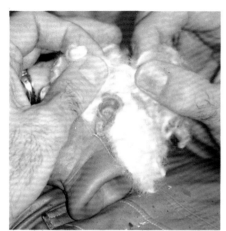

Applying second row of hair

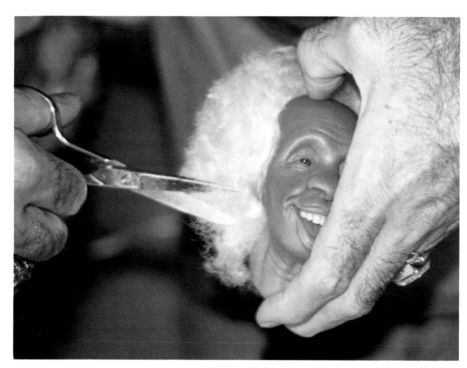

Trimming hair with scissors

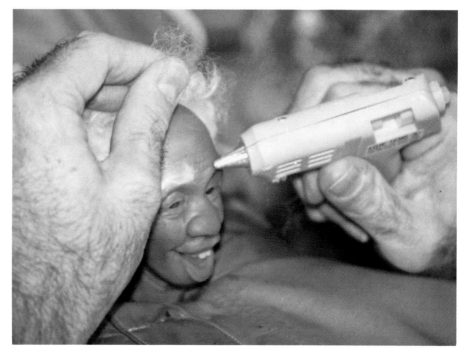

Applying eyebrows

use around the important areas like the face and set them aside. The other pieces will go on first. Make a 2 inch line with hot glue or other fast drying glue at the base of the occipital lobe. The line will go from the left ear to the center of the base of the occipital bone. As soon as the glue is placed, quickly attach the hair. Each strand will be placed side by side until you have made it across the head on to the right ear. Next, a line about 1/2 inch above that one does the same. Generally three to four lines cover the back of the head. Notice in the photograph, the next line of hair is placed running from the top of the temple to a spot in front of the left ear. This strand of hair makes the front edge of the sideburn and temporal hair. This is where you use your favorite piece of hair due to its curl, cut and shape.

Strands are now placed on the top of the head. Start at the crown, make a "U" shape on top of the head as shown. Place the hair coming forward from the crown to the frontal bone of the doll. Another strand of hair is placed in front of the "U" in the shape of an upside-down "D". This shape will form the hair for the top of the head and the widow's peak. The same is done for a lady or a man, but the lady's "D" extends completely across the front of the head, whereas a man's "D" is very narrow and just fits in the center of the head.

With the hair all in place now, we comb it out with a 3 inch needle. Much like you would comb out your own hair if you had a fresh perm. Work out the curls first; be gentle or the hair will pull out if you are too harsh. After you have combed it altogether you may style it anyway you like. I like to use a puff look on Santa and a tied-back look on my mountain men and cowboys. The Gibson girl look is as your skill will allow. After the hair is styled, I spray it with hair spray to keep it in shape. It is good to use a doll hairnet for shipping and storing the doll.

Surprise! If you have completed each of the steps to this point you have nearly finished your doll. Place all of the component pieces aside now so we can make the body.

CHAPTER 10

Sculpting the Body Stocking

SCULPTING THE BODY STOCKING

MATERIALS:

- Body stocking or enough double knit fabric to make one
- Scissors
- 14 gauge steel wire armature
- Vice grips
- One pound of polyfill
- Hemostats or needle-nose pliers
- A three inch needle
- Heavy-duty thread/button thread
- Hot glue gun or white glue
- Mohair wig or natural mohair braids

If you ever enjoyed making pillows or stuffed animals, you will love soft sculpting the body of your doll. Here you can nip and tuck away to improve your doll's appearance and add to its special character. Just as no two human bodies are exactly alike, each one-of-a-kind creation will sport its own unique body shape. Soft sculpted bodies are perfect for polymer dolls as they can be constructed quickly, shape nicely, are inexpensive to make, and pose easily.

Body Stocking

Although many doll artists use muslin, experience taught me that the best material for a body stocking is a quality double knit fabric that stretches in only one direction and will not run. Double knit is very giving and may be soft sculptured to fit your doll. Muslin on the other hand will not stretch and must be sewn with gussets and darts to make the shape of the doll. Another disadvantage to muslin is that it will not allow your doll to gesture as easily as a double knit

body. Not all double knits are the same, however. I searched for years to find just the right fabric. Once I found it, I bought enough for a full year's production for myself, plus extra to manufacture ready-made body stockings for sale. Take the time to shop around and experiment with different double knit fabrics until you find one that is just right for you.

The body stocking design is easy to make. The soft sculptured body for the doll illustrated in this section is an 18 inch cloth body. Just draw a basic body shape like the ones we drew as children when we were making those paper dolls all strung together, only this time construct it to the dimensions of your doll. Once you have designed the body stocking, cut out two exactly alike from your fabric and sew them together around the edge with a serger (overlock) or a straight stitch machine. In a pinch you can even hand sew it. After sewing the body together turn it inside out with the sewn seams inside the body stocking.

I am reminded here of a show I once attended back east where I found myself in desperate need of a doll body. But, I had no fabric, no armature, and no polyfill with me, which presented a huge problem. Thinking quickly, I pulled a knit polo shirt out of my suit case, cut it into a body stocking and hand sewed it together using the hotel mending kit. Then I built an armature from clothes hangers, and pulled the polyfill from my hotel pillow to stuff the body with. In short order I had completed my impromptu soft-sculptured body and imagined myself pretty clever for having accomplished

such a great feat. Only later did I learn that nearly every professional dollmaker admits to having improvised like that once or twice in their career.

Body Armature

Now your body stocking is ready for an armature. The body armature is as important to the doll as the skeleton is to a human. If the armature is well proportioned and gestured properly, the doll comes to life. Some dolls seem to have no life because they stand straight up with their arms hanging lifelessly to their sides. Avoid this stiffness at all costs. One of my students entered a doll at the New York Toy Fair and found that no one paid much attention to it. Even though it was a beautiful doll and very well crafted, it had no life to it. We quickly reposed it to add gesture and watched the piece jump to life. Not only did the audience start noticing the doll, the piece received a much coveted nomination for the Dolls Award of Excellence. More than once the right gesturing has made the difference between a nice piece and a great piece. You must allow for that flexibility from the beginning.

Ready-made body armatures come in various shapes and sizes and are constructed from such materials as steel wire, aluminum, copper, wood, and even plastic pop beads. The plastic pop beads are the most expensive, but I think they are the least desirable. They are strong but do not work well on realistic dolls, because they cannot bend at the joints as well as wire and therefore will not gesture as gracefully. They bend to about 110°, whereas wire armatures ben

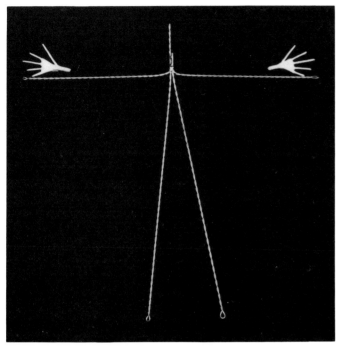

Body armature and hands armature

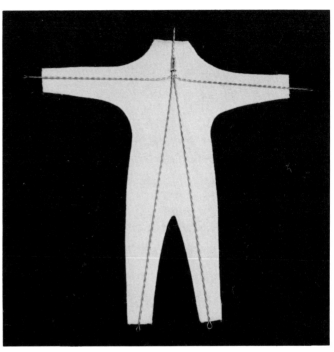

Body stocking with wire armatures

to a full 160°. This is a very important feature when gesturing the doll.

The most desirable and least expensive body armature is made of 14 gauge wire twisted together and locked at the neck to give it extra strength. As a practical matter, I would not spend valuable time making an armature because you can buy it ready-made for what it would cost you in time and materials to make your own. Keep in mind that whether you make your own or purchase one ready made, the armature must be fully posable and strong enough to hold the doll erect with all of its finished weight in place.

If you wish to make the armature, use 14 gauge steel wire. Make the length of

wire for the legs and body equal to the height of the doll minus the head and feet. Clamp two full length wires in a vice, attach a pair of vice grips to the other end. Spin the wire until it is tightly wrapped together creating a candy cane look. Notice how strong the wires

become once twisted together. In the illustration and photographs, you will also notice that one of the legs is made long enough to serve as the doll's neck. Now make both arms and place the arms and the legs together. Lastly, wrap a neck collar around the joint and solder

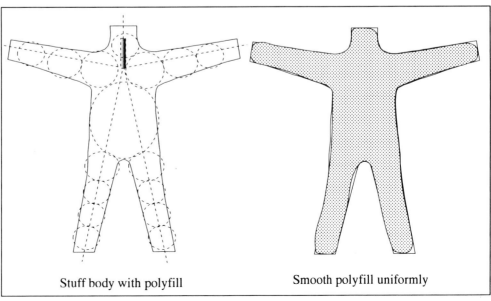

Stuff body with polyfill   Smooth polyfill uniformly

them together. If you have braising equipment, use that instead of soldering.

Stuffing the Body

Slip the completed armature inside the body of your doll and stuff with polyfill until the doll is firm. Be sure to place the same amount of fill on both sides of the wire so that you will not feel the wire once the doll is completed. After you have determined which part of the doll will be the front and the back, you may add additional stuffing in places such as the buttocks, breasts, and stomach. Hemostats or needle-nose pliers serve well in stuffing the different body parts. Just clamp onto a ball of fill and use the tool to insert it deep into the body cavity. If your doll is to be fat, this is the time to build up the stomach and hips.

Once the body is firmly stuffed, you may further adjust this stuffing under the body stocking by manipulating it with the 3 inch needle poked just under the fabric. Use this needle to push and pull the stuffing to desired shape. Work it until all unwanted lumps are smoothed throughout the entire body and low areas are properly filled out. When done, the doll should feel smooth and about as firm as your own unflexed leg.

Soft Sculpting

Now we will start the soft sculpting process. Using a 3 inch needle and heavy button hole thread, make a stitch and knot in the center of the crotch. Notice in

the illustration that the needle is threaded into the body and comes out about 3 inches up from the first knot in the crotch. Pull the needle out at the 3 inch point and then over the top of the body. Pull it tight and anchor it at the same place you started in the crotch. This will form a nice buttocks. You may make it as deep or as shallow as you like depending on the design and age of your doll. Using the same anchor point, stretch the thread under the left buttocks up to the side of the doll and anchor just below the waist. This new line will form the left buttock. Now go through the doll to the other side, anchor and go under the right buttock, anchor at the crotch. With the thread in place, use your 3 inch needle to manipulate the fill and better shape the buttocks. Work it until you have two nicely formed buttocks. This completes the buttocks area of the doll. If you have

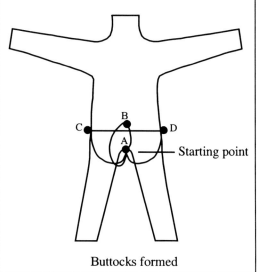

Buttocks formed

questions about this procedure, carefully study the illustrations and follow the example.

With the buttocks complete, form the waist by tying a knot on the right side of the body 1 inch above the side seam of the buttocks. Draw the thread across the back of the doll to the other side, pull tight and anchor. This forms a waistline across the back of the doll. You will be able to make the doll as fat or as thin as you desire

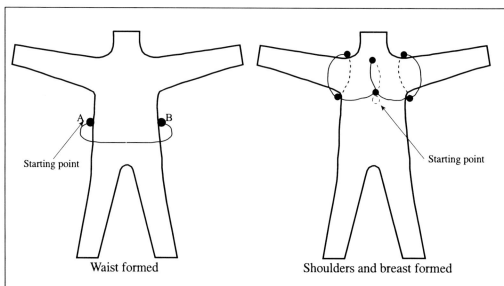

Waist formed

Shoulders and breast formed

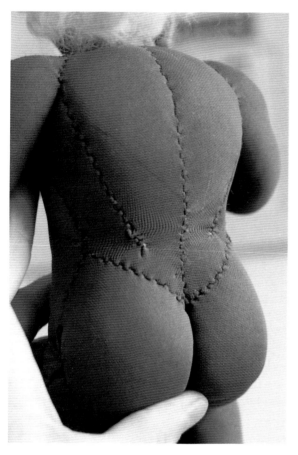

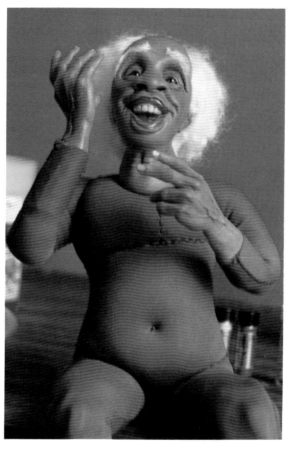

Far Left:
Completed
body showing
ladder stitch

Left:
Front of the body
finished

by adjusting the tension.

The shoulders are sculpted by first anchoring under the arms with a knot. Then draw the thread over the outside of the arm and insert the needle through the top of the shoulder (shown in the illustration). The reason for putting the needle through the material at the top of the shoulder is to keep it from slipping off the shoulder. Pull the thread down the back side of the arm and anchor it at the location of the first knot. The tighter you pull the thread the more definition you will see in the shoulders. After you have taken the thread around the shoulder and tied it off at the bottom, you may bend the wire armature at the shoulder. Make sure the shoulder wire is bent sharply down at a 90° angle. This simple adjustment creates beautifully squared shoulders.

To sculpt the breasts, use the same proceedure used for the buttocks. Anchor at the center of the back, pushing the needle through the body to the bottom of the rib cage in the front of the doll and anchor again. Now put the needle under the fabric and up to the top of the breast, at the trachea point between the collarbones. The same procedure is done for male and female. Pull the thread over the top of the material down to the anchor point at the bottom of the rib cage and pull the thread. The tighter you pull it, the deeper the cleavage and the more defined the breasts will become. If making a male doll, pull the thread lightly. For a large busted woman, pull the

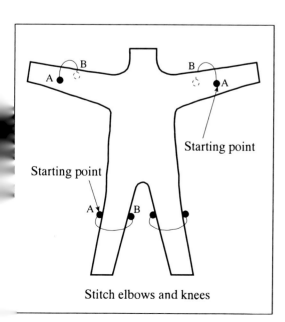

Stitch elbows and knees

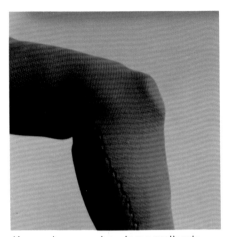

Knee close up showing prosthesis

thread tightly. Next, thrust the needle back into the body of the doll and come out just under the armpit on the right side. Anchor the thread and pull it down and around the right breast. This will allow you to make the breasts any size you like from a firm chest of a young male to the sagging breasts of an older female. If you wish to have realism showing through the clothing you may want to stitch in nipples. Upon completing the right breast, you may repeat the same procedure to form the left one. You

may choose to place additional balls of fill in the breasts, buttocks, and shoulders for greater definition. Once in place, manipulate the fill to desired shape and size with your 3 inch needle.

The crease in the arm at the elbow joint and the crease in the back of the leg at the knee is made in the same way. Start with the right arm, anchor the thread on the inside seam at the elbow, then pull the thread across the front of the arm to the other side and tie a knot. The tighter you pull the thread the more you can bend the arm (your choice). The left arm is completed by repeating the same procedure. The legs are done in the exact same manner only you pull the thread across the back of the leg instead of the front.

Other sculpting may be done to enhance your doll such as belly-button, elbow joints, rib cage, biceps, triceps and other muscle formations. Generally, if you are dressing the doll, the only sculpting you will need to do are the elements clearly defined in this chap-

ter. More advanced soft sculpting includes hiding stitches, building muscle tissue under the material of the body, and even adding hard sculpted body parts, such as knees elbows, and breast-plates. The sculptured breast-plate is useful if you wish to have the shirt open on a doll and expose the chest. In some cases you may choose to sculpt the legs and arms right to the hip or shoulder. If you do, continue to follow the directions above for soft sculpting the remainder of the body.

The last touch (this is for serious dollmakers) is to sew darts with a ladder stitch. Stitch the back, sleeves, shoulders, waist, buttocks, arms, legs, and the breasts. The ladder stitch goes from side to side forming darts as shown in the illustration. After making the darts, pull the thread tight to stitch it up. This may be done to any part of the body. One of the advantages of the ladder stitch is that it tailors the body to any desired shape with nearly an invisible stitch. Notice in the illustration, when you desire a wide place in the body, you stitch close together. For a narrow place like the waist, stitch widely. In the photo of the back of the finished doll note how the stitch nearly disappears and how it tailors the body together.

This stitch is one of my favorite parts of making the doll. When finished, place a running stitch around the neck and pull it tight. The head fits over the top of the body and onto the armature sticking out of the body.

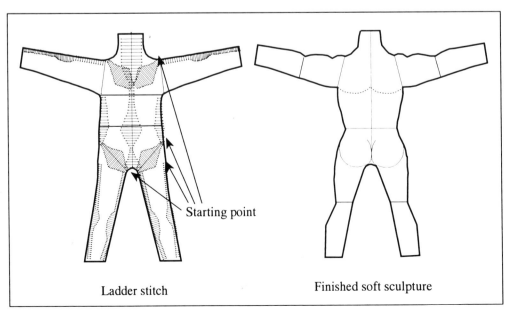

Ladder stitch   Finished soft sculpture

Starting point

Putting the Doll Together

Now comes the fun part of putting all the components of your doll together. The head, hands and legs are attached to the body by first drilling a ¹/₈ inch hole in the center of the base of each appendage. You will attach the head to the shoulders using hot glue. Since the hot glue dries almost instantly, you must work quickly.

Determine ahead of time whether the head should be looking up, down, or to one side or the other. Be sure of exactly how you want it before you start gluing, because once the head is glued on, you cannot change it. Then quickly place a line of glue around the base of the neck and on the neck armature wire. Immediately push the head down firmly on the body in the desired position.

The arms and the legs are attached in a similar manner. Place the hot glue on the armature and immediately stick it in the arm or leg hole. Allow three minutes for the glue to completely cool. Pull the sleeve down around the arm and fold the sleeve under to give it a nice edge. Place a ring of hot glue around the arm and pull the sleeve down over the glue. Hold in place and allow it to cool. The body stocking may serve as long underwear if you like. If this is the case, you may want to run a bodice around the bottom of the sleeve to give it a finished look. The same process is used for the other arm and the legs. Plan ahead when placing the arms and legs into position to assure the hands are facing the direction you desire (i.e. palm up or down).

As strange as it may sound, I should also tell you the thumbs point to the front of the doll and so do the toes. Obviously you know your right from your left and your front from your back, but believe me, when putting a doll together it is entirely possible to make these mistakes. In every class I teach, someone puts the feet on backwards, the hands on the wrong side, or ends up with two left hands.

With the head, arms, and legs securely attached to the doll, you may now proceed with dressing the doll. Place the doll in an upright position on a doll stand to help judge the proportions when designing the clothing. This way the doll serves as a mannequin while you create its costume.

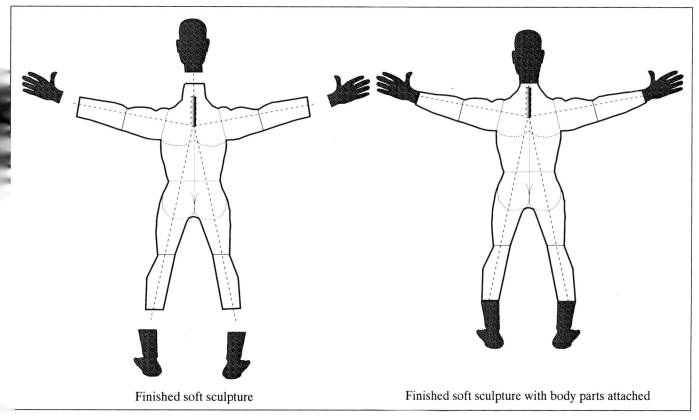

Finished soft sculpture   Finished soft sculpture with body parts attached

Abdomen and chest finished

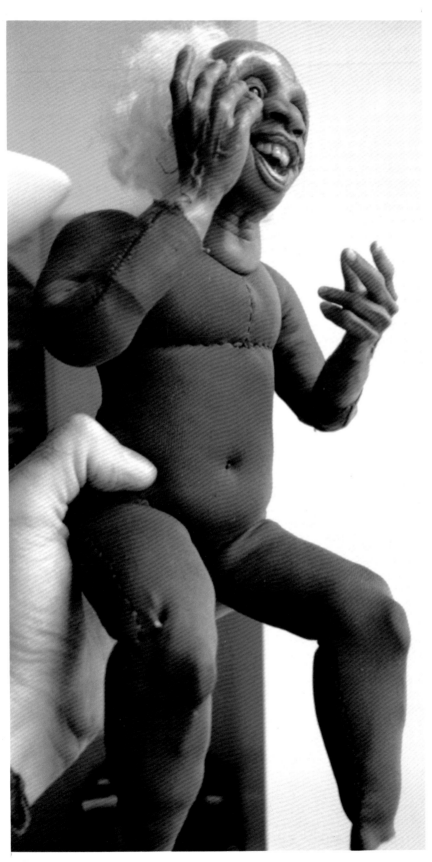

CHAPTER 11

Dressing & Accessorizing the Doll

"Holy Man" 21" Cernit doll by Jack

From the frilly ruffles of a lady's canteen costume to the patched coveralls of an old field hand, dressing and accessorizing the doll can be the most exciting part of dollmaking. As yours is a one-of-a-kind doll, you are limited in costuming only by your imagination and your talents. You can fashion creations as simple or as complicated as your character demands. But do not count on finding ready-made costumes unless you have sculpted a child or a baby doll. In that case you might be able to find an acceptable outfit right off the rack, with little or no adjustments. On the other hand, creating a character as unique as Winston Churchill, requires expertly sewn clothing made either by yourself or a professional costume maker. Costumes for less demanding characters may simply be glued. The choice is yours.

Remember, NIADA's definition of a doll says it should "appear" to be undressable. With this in mind let me assure you that many one-of-a-kind dolls are indeed glued together. Nearly all of mine are glued and I suggest that for the most part, you glue your costumes as well. With glue the pants fit tight and the shirts fit perfectly at the neck and wrists. Even the jackets can be tailored with glue. Clothing glued together is made just exactly as you would if you were to stitch it together. But of course, it will not come off. There are many different fabric glues on the market. You will be able to choose from several types at your local fabric or craft store, or you may use your hot glue gun. I prefer the hot glue gun because I like to work quickly. It is tricky

"The Jazz Player" 21" Cernit doll made by Jack for the 1991 NIADA convention in New Orleans. The accessories such as the coins, bottles, bottle case and the bench, are all available through miniature shops. This doll is kept in the permanent collection of Jack Johnston, as it is the first sitting doll he made.

Above:
"The Cowboy." This 20" Cernit cowboy is holding an authentic guitar and sitting near a leather handmade saddle.

Left:
"The Fisherman." Notice the backdrop is a real pier and boats, an effect made by photographing the doll and the background through a 200mm lens.

though, in that you must plan ahead and know exactly how the entire costume fits together before you begin. Once you apply the hot glue, it is there for good. One wrong move could easily ruin an entire costume. With fabric glue, you have a little more flexibility because it takes a while to dry. If something did not work out quite right, this slow drying process gives you the opportunity to change or adjust the costume. I suggest that you take the time to experiment beforehand with different methods, glues, and fabrics to determine which works best for you.

For those occasions when sewing is required to complete a costume, I prefer to design the costume myself first and then have the clothing made by a qualified seamstress or costume maker as described earlier in Chapter 4. I should tell those of you who are talented seamstresses or tailors, that for those extenuating circumstances when sewing is a must, there are definite advantages to sewing the costume yourself. These range from having more control to a much better fit at a fraction of the cost. For custom-made costumes you may pay as little as $25.00 for a simple dress or as much as several hundred for a man's suit, depending on its complexities. The following photographs show two undressable suits that fit extremely well, but they were expensive ($250 for Winston and $350 for Mark Twain). Expense is relative though. If you plan to sell your one-of-a-kind doll for several thousand, then $350 for a suit is pretty reasonable.

"Mark Twain"

When selling a doll to a doll reproduction company it becomes essential to have costumes that are removable, yet fit with perfection. For example, even though Norman Rockwell's costume of casual workclothes was quite simple and would have been easy for me to make with glue and a bit of sewing, I had to have the clothes tailor made, because the doll needed to be fully undressable. When gluing a doll's clothing together, it becomes glued onto the doll forever and is therefore undressable unless you destroy the doll. What made "Norman Rockwell" an exception was the fact that Franklin Mint bought the doll for the purpose of reproduction, which necessitated taking him apart for the molds to be made. That would have been fine, were it not for the fact that the original is a museum piece and needed to be reassembled, re-costumed, and placed

"Winston Churchill," this Cernit doll was commissioned for Phil and Peggy Crosby and is kept in their permanent collection in Winter Park, Florida. The costume was made from a life-size pattern by a Chinese tailor. All of the pockets and buttons work. The watch is a real gold watch that keeps time. The hat and cane are made of Cernit.

"Norman Rockwell's Triple Self Portrait," 21" Cernit doll done by Jack for the 100 year birthday party. This doll is featured in the centerfold of the November 1994 issue of *Contemporary Doll Collector*. The doll is now owned by Franklin Mint. Jack considers this one of his best sculptures to date.

back in the museum in its perfect form for others to enjoy.

Designing Your Costumes

Designing your doll's outfits often calls for hours of period research to assure authenticity, which of course adds to the value and realism of the doll. This research may be conducted through history books, costume design books, old photographs and postcards, or by trips to a museum. When studying an era, pay attention not only to the style of the costume, but to all the details such as the types of materials used, the prints, the kind of buttons or belts, and the style of hats and undergarments for that period of time. Also note what type of character wore these clothes and what were they doing when they wore them. Consider the class and cultural differences as well. Remember, you are not just dressing a doll, you are creating a character and everything you put on him should say something about who he is. Just as you make a statement with your own choice of clothing, dress your character as if he too were making a statement.

In designing your one-of-a-kind costumes, one should always plan on as many realistic features as plausible, such as usable buttons and working zippers and flies. These features not only enhance your costume, they make dressing and undressing the doll much easier.

Crafting Your Patterns

In some cases you will be able to buy pre-drawn patterns for your costume. In others you may have to design your own. Pattern making can be easy and fun even if you have never made one before. Just use the finished doll as a mannequin for your pattern. You may use pattern tissue, tissue paper, newspaper, or even paper towels to draw your pattern. The dimensions you will take directly from the measurements of your doll. If you feel you need a little extra help with this, there are several good books available on pattern making that take you through the step-by-step process.

Always consider scale when planning a costume for your character. Everything you do is part of the whole look and it all needs to work together. To assure that the doll looks in scale, choosing the right fabric, buttons, prints and patterns is imperative. The fabric, for example, must be a very tight weave for a doll this size—something like a tightly woven linen. This may cost a little more, but the look is well worth the additional expense.

Choosing the Right Materials

Prints or stripes in the cloth for your doll's costume must be in scale. Large prints will look out of proportion to the scale of the doll, whereas small prints will enhance the design and finish the doll correctly. For example, you would not dress yourself in material with polka dots the size of saucers or flowers as big as melons. Therefore, be sure that polka dots or flowers on the print you choose for your doll's costume would not be proportionately that large. Finding small prints is a challenge, but they are available, keep looking. When you find them, buy plenty to use for later costumes, or for trade with fellow dollmakers.

Button Making

Fasteners such as buttons, snaps and hooks must be in scale as well. These items are also available commercially if you look hard enough. Buttons are my favorite. I think they finish off a garment very nicely. The right buttons add decorative touch to your costume. Through the years, buttons have been made out of many different materials such as plastic, glass, ceramics, pearls, semi-precious stones, crystals, metal, and even wood. If finding the right size or style buttons for your costume proves too difficult or time consuming, you may easily make your own out of clay, metal, or wood.

To make a button out of clay, first determine the look that best fits the costume and the exact size of the button you wish to make. With that in mind, roll a small ball

Metal buttons serve the costume and the character.

of clay from the color of your choice and cut a button disk out of the roll. A simple pattern may be etched into the button if you wish. Then put two holes in the disk and place it in the oven. When making buttons out of polymer clay, you should fire them at a higher temperature than normal (as high as 265°). This additional temperature may turn the buttons tan in color, but they will be much stronger than the normal 250°. Discoloration to the button will not affect it adversely. In fact, yellow or tan buttons look very natural.

In some cases metal buttons more appropriately serve the costume and the character as illustrated in this Santa Claus. To fashion brass buttons, begin by selecting a brass rod the thickness you wish your button to be. Cut the button disks off of the end of the rod and

drill two tiny holes in them. You may also wish to lightly tap in some ornamentation on the button as well, before you polish it up and sew it on. Because these buttons are brass, they will be very strong and will look great on the doll.

Wooden buttons may be cut off the end of wooden dowels. Drill in two small holes and paint, varnish or decorate appropriately for the outfit. Do not be afraid to have fun with your buttons. In previous years people made an art out of decorating buttons. Some became quite elaborate as button collectors can testify. Consider your costume and your character.

Accessories

Accessories often make or break the doll. We have probably all seen a wonderful doll displayed with illchosen accessories that have destroyed the overall effect of the doll. I've seen it all too many times. Knowing the amount of work that went into crafting such a fine doll, why would the artist spend any less time accessorizing it. The wrong accessories or those out of scale can seriously hurt your piece. For example, if you have a child sitting on a chair that is out of scale it hurts the value of the doll. By the same token, if you have a chair custommade for that doll in the right style, shape, color, and size, it reinforces the statement you want your doll to make. This can increase the value of the doll. In my opinion, you may even double the price of the doll if you have accessories that fit the motif.

Accessories need not be expensive. Such things as the wonderful

Left:
"Tara Jane," a three-quarter life size doll made after Jack's daughter Tara Jane Johnston. It is now sold as a mold through Bell Ceramics of Clermont, Florida.

Below:
"Christmas Alone," this 21" doll was sculpted by Jack. Notice it is holding an authentic newspaper. This paper is an antique, printed by a newspaper company as a salesman sample. (A very rare find.)

lantern shown on page 25 with the Mark Twain doll, only cost one dollar. Though it looks authentic and highly effective, it is merely a pencil sharpener made of plastic. Because it looks so realistic and fits the scale of two inches equals one foot, it works. On the other hand, your doll may require a more sophisticated specialized accessory which you may need to have custommade as in the case of Mark Twain's desk.

In the photo of "Norman Rockwell's Triple Self Portrait" you can see that the right furniture and accessories actually make the doll what it is. Its authenticity is

"The Boat Maker." The table, chair, boat and tools are made in scale to fit the doll.

"The Toy Maker," this doll is in the permanent collection of Jack Johnston.

without question. I made certain of that during the six months I spent researching the accessories for Norman. I traveled to the Rockwell Museum in Stockbridge, Massachusetts, on five different occasions to study Mr. Rockwell's work, his easel, chair, palette, and even his garbage can. Notice in the two photographs placed side by side that every detail is in the doll vignette. There are over 100 pieces in this scene, from his pipe, right down to his eight adjustable wing nut screws holding the easel together. The easel actually works. It adjusts up and down, forward and back, and is made of the same

"The Music Man," this 28" Cernit doll was sculpted by Jack for the Disney World Doll and Teddy Bear Show of 1991.

PHOTOGRAPHED BY: RUSS ROBISON PHOTOGRAPHY

"Norman Rockwell with Jack Johnston," this photograph shows the size of the doll in relationship to its maker.

"The Doll Maker," this 28" Cernit doll was sculpted by Jack for Bell Ceramics. It was made into a mold for porcelain dollmaking. It is one of the most popular Bell molds. The original is kept in the permanent collection of Bell Ceramics in Clermont, Florida.

wood as the original. The mirror is handmade to exact scale of the original painting.

One of the intriguing differences in my doll and Mr. Rockwell's painting (besides the obvious fact that he is a master and I am a beginner) is that the sculpture may be seen from all angles. When I finished the piece and delivered it to the Rockwell Museum in Stockbridge, the workers could not keep from looking at the back side of the work. I suggested to them that they stand in front of the mirror to get the full effect of the design. They told me that they had seen that view since the painting was completed in 1963, now they were enjoying a side they had never seen.

On a more personal note, I would like to add that making the art form of "Norman Rockwell" has been the most artistically satisfying thing I have ever done. I grew up loving his work, in fact his work is what made me want to be an artist. I have followed his work from the age of eight. I remember seeing his illustrations in the *Saturday Evening Post*, and even cutting them out and putting them on the wall of my bedroom. All this goes to say that if you

choose to sculpt characters that you can relate to, that you feel you know and love, this feeling will show in your work and elevate you to a new level of sculpting.

CHAPTER 12

Develop a Marketing &
Business Plan

DEVELOP A MARKETING & BUSINESS PLAN

Think It Through

The key element to a successful dollmaking business is a well thought out marketing plan. No matter how beautiful your dolls are, if you cannot sell them, you are only stocking your own private museum. Selling your work is what marketing is all about. Many doll artist make the mistake of thinking that talent takes care of itself and guarantees success. Nothing could be further from fact. Many great artists armed with only talent never reach notoriety or ever successfully sell their work, whereas many others with less talent but better marketing skills and a good business plan, soar to the top.

After serving as a marketing consultant for over 25 years, I feel that I have a fairly good handle on the marketing of a product and can share some valuable tips. Marketing is not a science, it is an art that can and must be learned if you are to succeed. To do so requires comprehensive research and study. You must acquire a working knowledge of what you can and cannot do in the marketplace. Even if you have little or no present knowledge of marketing, you can succeed by carefully adhering to the guidelines set forth in this chapter. Some of the ideas presented may seem very basic and others complicated. The purpose of this chapter is not to discourage or overwhelm you, but rather to give you direction and perhaps prevent a disaster before it occurs. As with any new business venture, you must enter it with both eyes wide open. Although marketing involves all aspects of the business world, I will zero in on what you can do to target the doll/craft industry.

By definition, marketing is the combined ability to:

- Identify the exact groups of people to whom you wish to sell
- Get the right information out to them
- Motivate them to buy from you

Determine Your Market

Now that you know how to design, sculpt, costume, and accessorize beautiful dolls, you must find your potential customers and convince them that you are the doll artist who can supply what they want. To do this you need to determine the market for your product. This may be done by the simple method I employed. First, have a quality 4"x 5" photograph taken of your dolls. Any good photographer will have the equipment to produce these for you. The photos are not cheap, but they should offer the best most professional representation of your work. Choose one or two of these and have them reproduced in 5"x 7" prints. Then mail these out to targeted shops around America for a sampling. A letter must accompany the photos explaining that these dolls are prototypes and will be on the market within the next few months. Let the shop owners know that he or she is part of a market research program. Ask the owners how much they would expect to pay for these limited edition, one-of-a-kind, or mass-produced dolls. Further, after determining how much they would expect to pay, ask how many they would order when the dolls become available.

Inquire as to whether they like the way the dolls are dressed, accessorized, painted, etc. Ask what changes they would make if they could. This is one of the most productive studies you could ever make, but it can also be one of the cruelest. You will have to accept the answers you get, but isn't it better to know that the dolls are not well received in the test market, rather than going into full production and then find out the dolls have no audience appeal. If the dolls get great reviews, then go ahead and target the market.

Targeting the Market

After you complete your sample study, collect the data and separate it into categories. If the dolls were well received and the suggested price point is in the upper level, then go for the top quality wholesale marketing shows. Keep your price up and do not discount below wholesale. The targets for upscale dolls are the best collectible shops in America. All of these shops are represented at the major market shows in America. The three best shows to attend are the Anaheim show in California, the IDEX show (wherever it happens to be in its rotating schedule) and the American International Toy Fair in New York. There are other less notable shows that are good, but if your dolls are "hot" they will sell out at these three shows. If they are really "hot" they will sell out at just one of them.

Analyze Your Competition

There is a certain amount of finesse involved when "shopping" your competitor. The term shopping means finding out as much as you can from your competitor without divulging who you are or why you are asking so many questions. Call the artist or his agent and ask the following questions:

- Do you have doll X for sale?
- How much is it selling for retail (you can figure whole sale and distributor)?
- How large is the edition?
- What are the accessories and how is it costumed?
- Is it manufactured in the US or overseas; if overseas by whom?
- What is the delivery date?
- Are they supplementing the advertising or placing ads on their own?
- Do they have a follow-up design? What is it? When will it be out? How much?
- Who is your greatest competition; how much is their doll selling for?

I recommend shopping every major competitor, itemizing all of the information into columns and then totaling the columns and figuring out averages. After you are armed with this data, you are ready to develop your company image.

Image

In this highly competitive industry there are thousands of doll artists all vying for the collector's attention. Your competition constantly floods the market with information on new dolls and doll related products. This means that to be noticed, you must somehow stand out amidst this deluge of information so that your customers can find you. Therefore, it is critical that you enter the market with an image that is consistent with the

message you wish to convey.

Developing your company image should be done with much thought and great care. Consider things like your long-term goals and growth potential. You would not want to establish yourself exclusively as a one-of-a-kind doll artist, if you hope to produce limited editions or turn to mold making in the near future. Allow flexibility for growth. Next you must identify what sets you apart from other dollmakers and be able to state it in one or two sentences. Study your target market to learn what would appeal to them. From this summary you can build an entire marketing campaign.

Once your company image is firmly entrenched in your mind, move to paper and reflect that image in your company name, business cards, letterhead, logo, slogan, and any printed material or advertisements (be sure to check any name for trademark infringement before committing to it). If you design all your publicity materials with your overall image in mind, each piece then works together sending out the same strong, consistent message. Even if you do not wish to invest in all these material initially, you must still plan them out for future use. This ensures that further down the road each added piece of publicity will continue to reinforce your overall image.

After you nail down a solid image back it up. For example, if you want to convey the warm image of a one-person home-based business, you must create a company name and logo that reflects this warmth. If you desire the larger, well-established business

image, reinforce that image in your logo and slogan. Remember that the way you present yourself to the market is the single most important factor in how the world perceives you.

Setting and Reaching Your Goals

Nearly all of us have set goals or objectives in our lives at one point or another to help us accomplish certain things. Goals are a method of measuring our improvement. You have probably set and reached several goals during your dollmaking sessions. Now more than ever it is important to really understand the goal setting process, because the key to any effective marketing/business plan is to learn to set, track and achieve your goals. Paul H. Dunn said, "When performance is measured it improves, when it is measured and reported back the rate of improvement accelerates." Now that you have a dollmaking business and marketing plan in mind, commit it to written goals that you can track and refer to often. They should be realistic, achievable and meaningful. Success Motivation Institute has as its motto, "Perception makes reality, what the mind can conceive it can achieve." Set your goals with the belief that you can achieve them and work at it everyday to ensure that you do.

Always set goals that are attainable and challenge yourself to reach them within a set time frame. Accept nothing less of yourself than your very best efforts. Once you have reached one goal, reward yourself. As you meet each goal, challenge yourself further by extending them. Eventually you will find yourself attaining goals that you never would have been able to reach, had you not successfully climbed each step of your goal ladder, one rung at a time.

Personal goals, business goals, and marketing goals should all be separate. The reason for this is self-preservation. If one were to fail, it would not necessarily affect the others. When you set goals you should always have a fall back plan in readiness. This is not meant to build in failure, but to have an acceptable alternate plan ready to implement. ⇨

List your personal and business goals for each separate week in the following manner:

MONDAY:
TUESDAY:
WEDNESDAY:
THURSDAY:
FRIDAY:
SATURDAY:
SUNDAY:
List your personal and business goals for this month:

List your personal and business goals for this year:

List your personal and business goals to be achieved in the next five years:

FIRST:

SECOND:

THIRD:

FOURTH:

FIFTH:

Marketing goals for the month:

Marketing goals for the year:

Marketing goals to be complete within five years:

Business and Marketing Plan

A business and marketing plan is essential to large scale marketing. The general purpose of a written plan is to clearly define where you are going and how you are going to get there. If you are going to sell small editions of dolls, then it will not be essential but still a good idea. Take the time to draft one up. By committing it to paper, you clearly set forth the direction of your business. It may also serve as a guide to be shared with employees, accountants, business associates and, last but not least, your banker. A solid business/marketing plan helps assure that everyone involved in the sales effort of your dolls, is singing off the same sheet of music. In it you should state the purpose of the business and the scope of your plan. The following is a sample business plan outline which I used in developing my plan.

SAMPLE BUSINESS PLAN OUTLINE

I.   Introduction and brief synopsis of your business
    A. State who you are and why you are qualified
    B. Describe your business

II. Marketing strategy
    A. Identify media outlets/how you plan to use
    B. Design timetable for press releases, etc.

III. Production Schedule and Scope
    A. Schedule for first year's production
    B. Total gross earnings first year

IV. Costs and Profits
    A. Cost breakdown per doll
    B. Profit margin per doll

V.   Venture Capital Requirements
    A. List operating expenses
    B. Venture capital required

VI. Competition/Opportunities
    A. Who they are
    B. How you plan to compete and beat

VII. Promotions
    A. Plan to project company image
    B. Public relations goals

VII. Summation
    A. What your research has determined
    B. Why you believe you can succeed

Pricing and Distribution

Pricing the doll is easy if you follow some simple steps. To help you better understand pricing and distribution, I have broken it down into six categories. These are the methods I use to price and sell my dolls.

Pricing

Pricing the dolls is done by counting the hours you have in producing the dolls, then assign a dollar per hour value to your work. Total the costs of costuming and accessories and add that to your hourly rate. With the two major costs added together, add any cost for advertising, shipping, travel, promotion, and general and administrative etc. For the purpose of clarity lets say the following numbers were totaled:

Hours (40) at $10. 00 per hour	$400.00
Costuming & Accessories	100.00
Shipping	15.00
Travel	35.00
Promotion	50.00
General and administrative (overhead)	100.00
Total	$700.00

Direct Sales

The best and cheapest way to sell your dolls is direct to the consumer. This is generally the first method used by new dollmakers. If the cost of the doll is $700.00 you may sell the doll for that price.

Retail Sales

Once you get too busy to sell your dolls yourself you will likely want to use a retail store. Merchants will need to mark your doll up by 100% (keystoning). This will put your doll at a selling price of $1,400.

Distributor Sales

The larger you get the less time you will have to spend with the sales effort; therefore, you will need to move up to the next logical step in the marketing ladder—that of distributor sales. The distributor will sell to retailers across America. For this service he will charge an additional 25%. This takes the price of your doll to $875.00.

The distributor now sells the doll to the retailer who marks it up 100% to $1,750.00.

Predatory Pricing

I have chosen to name the larger markup of the dolls predatory pricing. This means I kept all of the price in your doll for labor, materials, etc., and then I mark it up to meet the competition. Later you will be able to mark it up to the price your reputation will draw. For example, after you have been selling your dolls for a number of years, won all of the major awards, and have been written about in every national magazine, you will be able to double or even quadruple your price just because of your name. But, you must wait until you have paid your dues.

Intrinsic Value Pricing

As your dolls get better and your name begins to spread, the manufacturers will come to you to produce your dolls in volume. Obviously you would not want to sell them the rights to the same doll as mentioned above for $700.00. In this case you will make sure you cover all of your expenses and everything you would ever make on the doll. Therefore, a fair price for your doll may be $10,000.00 plus royalties. The royalties paid by most manufacturers on reproduction porcelain dolls vary from one-half to one percent to as high as three percent. This variation depends on how big your name is and how bad the manufacturer wants it. My only advice to you in the negotiation process is to negotiate with more than one manufacturer when you decide to sell your doll. None of the companies publish their royalty fees, therefore, you must shop around and make your best deal. Never sell your doll to the first offer and always let the company you are negotiating with know you are negotiating with another company at the same time (trust me on this one).

Advertising and Promotions

Making Use of the Media . . .
The effort to make the public aware of your product can generally be done without cost if you are creative. The biggest and most effective advertising campaigns have always been free. This is accomplished by carefully and strategically placing information about your product in the right place at the right time.

If your acting career needs a boost, "slap a cop." If you want to write a book let a "cop slap you." The old adage of all news reporters is; "dog bites man," is not a story, but "man bites dog," sells. For your story to be worthy of free publicity you must include information that is different or in some way contains a human interest angle.

Newspapers, magazines and electronic media offer the fastest route to notoriety. The power of the press is staggering. How many people have become famous overnight just because their face appeared on the 10:00 news? News sells! I'm not suggesting that you "slap a cop" or "bite a dog," but if you have a human interest angle to your story, by all means tell it. Everyone has something different or unique about themselves or their product. Identify and list those differences and specialties. Then identify media outlets who might be interested in your particular story and *sell yourself.*

The Press Release. . . Now that you have identified what makes your company news worthy tell it

in a press release. A basic press release is nothing more than a way to convey information to the media and other organizations. If you follow the traditional industry format for writing the press release, you will make it easier for journalists to determine that you have something of interest to them. Speak their language.

Your press release must include a contact name, phone number, and a suitable release date. It must be short and to the point. Most importantly you must include the five "W's"—*Who, What, When, Where* and *Why* (and/or *How*). You should also be aware that your release may be used word for word as you write it so make sure you supply enough information to "hook" both the news staff and the public. Say just enough to pique their interest, but always leave the reader wanting more!

Industry Awareness . . . Trade journals are constantly looking for good information about new products or new talent in the marketplace. If you have a good story, tell it to the trades. They might publish your article along with photos. And believe me, it can make a career.

When contacting the trades, make sure your information is accurate, documented, and professional. Nothing is more harmful to your chances of being published than to pump up your product to the editors and then follow up that initial contact with poor photographs and flawed descriptions.

To assist you in becoming, published I offer a few simple tips. First determine which trade magazine you would like to be published in, then study the artist profiles in current and back issues of that publication. Look for things like how many words the average profile story runs, the type of artwork that accompanies each article, the writing style and flavor, the type face, and the different human interest and artistic angles. Ask yourself what drew the editor's attention to those particular artists and what those same editors might like about your work. After you have analyzed the articles, you should be able to draft up your own in a similar style.

The clincher is to send in professional quality 4" x 5" transparencies to accompany the article as discussed earlier in this book. The doll and craft magazines are continuously looking for good information on new artists and/or dollmaking techniques. If you have the article and back it up with quality photography, you can grab their attention.

If the thought of writing your own story and photographing your own dolls strikes a cord of terror, do not despair. There are professionals in those fields who can help. Have your dolls photographed in a professional studio and hire a free-lance writer to draft up a story for you. Often if you send in pictures of your work along with a convincing letter on why a magazine should feature you, they will assign a staff writer to interview you and write your article. In either case you must draft up the initial contact letter much like a news brief and really sell yourself to the editors.

Mention any awards and recogitions, and the slant you think your story should take. What makes your story worthy of the space in their magazine? Don't be shy! You have everything to gain and nothing to lose, so give it your best shot.

If the media or trade magazines show no interest in your work after your first attempt, don't give up. Query them again with a different slant. Remember, it is the squeaky wheel that gets greased. If they do publish your story, write them a nice letter to express your thanks. Send them additional information periodically as your business progresses. The readership and editors love follow-up stories.

Craft and Trade Shows . . .
One inexpensive way to market your product is through local craft and trade shows. These shows offer several advantages for the small business person. They are as follows:

- minimal expenses
- elaborate exhibits not required
- close to home
- provide immediate income
- offer instant market research
- expose you and your product
- offer opportunity to view the competition
- often have media coverage

The Brochure . . . Produce a brochure, even if it's a simple one. When using brochures, more than with almost any other medium, your product will be compared closely with your competitors'. Keep in mind the objectives you want to accomplish and focus the brochure appropriately. Like all of your publicity material great thought and care should go into

the statement your brochure makes. Be certain that it portrays the correct image of your company and represents your work in the most flattering manner.

Your local printer can give you ideas on style and form and help you to design a quality brochure to represent your work. Include the following:

- quality photography
- accurate, informative text
- quality type and paper stock

Company brochures can be used as mailers and/or handouts at trade shows. They also carry a strong professional message when sent to magazine editors. Detail what makes your work special. Transform the features of your dolls and company into benefits for the collectors. If you want prospective buyers to hang on to your brochure, make it attractive and include valuable information and useful advice (checklists, comparison charts, secondary market information, calendars, etc.).

Newsletters . . . Communication ranks high on the list of tools we have to make an impression on the consumer. I keep in touch with my collectors through a newsletter. I let them know on a semi-annual basis what I am currently doing and how they can be a part of it. Buyers are always excited to hear about the artist's success. If you receive good press or win awards, your prices are going to go up. Owners of your work need and want to know about this. They may even want to add more of your work to their collection. The following list of information should be included in the typical doll artist's newsletter.

- new information about your dolls
- news about how they benefited someone else
- new or increased prices reflecting additional value
- upcoming events that effect your collectors
- highlight one of your collectors
- include a calendar of your business related events
- showcase additional dolls or related products
- thank your collectors for their support

A well-crafted newsletter builds the perception that you care about your collectors enough to go the extra mile. Again, if you feel uncomfortable writing this yourself, consider enlisting the help of your support team. Perhaps a collector or someone from your local doll club with writing skills would be willing to donate their time to help you make use of this valuable tool.

Follow-Up and Referrals . . . The best way to promote your business is with satisfied, happy customers. Through timely and meaningful follow-up you will keep your customers happy and at the same time earn the right to ask for a referral. It is entirely appropriate to write to your doll owners once or twice a year (assuming you keep them happy) and ask them for names of friends who you may contact about your business. To those whose referrals resulted in a new sale, I often offer half price off on a seminar or give a discount on their next purchase. Keep in mind that business generated from referrals didn't cost you a dime in advertising. If people like your work and believe in your product, they are usually happy to help spread the word and tell their family and friends about you.

Paid Advertisements . . . With the high costs of advertising in today's market, few of us can afford a shotgun approach or apply a hit-or-miss attitude. Today marketing costs may exceed 30% of production cost. Being off in your calculations and projections by just 20% could destroy your ability to realize a profit. Believe me, no one is 100% accurate in their marketing projections, but we do attempt to project as closely as possible to actual costs. The professional's struggle to be within the range of 20% to 30% cost of marketing. If you exceed 30%, you are out of business.

Consider this. The cost of producing a doll is generally 30%, marketing costs also projects to 30%, and general and administrative overhead falls somewhere around 10%. That leaves 30% for profit. It now becomes evident that if your ad campaign and production vary by 15% each, your profit is gone. These sobering figures force us to become highly selective in the type of paid advertising we choose.

For maximum effectiveness at minimum cost, shop around. There are many magazines in the doll industry to choose from. A trip to your local library can produce a list of all the industry related publications. For the price of a sheet of paper and a stamp you can send for their price lists and choose the type and size ad that best suits your budget, from small one-inch classifieds to full page color ads.

NOTES